PYGMALION
GROWS
UP

Research on Teaching Monograph Series

PUBLISHED

Student Characteristics and Teaching by Jere E. Brophy and Carolyn M. Evertson

Pygmalion Grows Up: Studies in the Expectation Communication Process by Harris M. Cooper and Thomas L. Good

The Invisible Culture by Susan Urmston Philips

FORTHCOMING IN 1983

Active Mathematics Instruction by Thomas L. Good and Douglas Grouws

Cooperative Learning by Robert E. Slavin

Staff Networking in Secondary Schools by Philip Cusick

Class Size and Instruction: A Field Study (tentative title) by Leonard S. Cahen, Nikola Filby, Gail McCutcheon, and Diane Kyle

PYGMALION GROWS UP

STUDIES IN THE EXPECTATION COMMUNICATION PROCESS

Harris M. Cooper
Thomas L. Good
THE CENTER FOR RESEARCH
IN SOCIAL BEHAVIOR

Longman
New York & London

Pygmalion Grows Up
Studies in the Expectation Communication Process

Longman Inc., 1560 Broadway, New York, N.Y. 10036
Associated companies, branches, and representatives
throughout the world.

Developmental Editor: Lane Akers
Editorial and Design Supervisor: Joan Matthews
Production Supervisor: Ferne Y. Kawahara
Manufacturing Supervisor: Marion Hess

Library of Congress Cataloging in Publication Data

Cooper, Harris M.
  Pygmalion grows up.

  (Research on teaching monograph series)
  Bibliography: p.
  1. Interaction analysis in education.
2. Expectation (Psychology) 3. Academic achievement. 4. Classroom environment—Psychological
aspects. I. Good, Thomas L., 1943–
II. Title. III. Series.
LB1084.C57 1983   370.15′3   82–14876
ISBN 0-582-28401-5

Manufactured in the United States of America

Contents

Figures and Tables

FIGURES

TABLES

Preface

Few social experiments have captured as much public attention as Rosenthal and Jacobson's *Pygmalion in the Classroom* (1968). The results of *Pygmalion* were salient and controversial because they suggested that the performance expectations of classroom teachers might serve as powerful influences (positive or negative) on the achievement of students. The implications of *Pygmalion's* results for minority pupils and children from low SES backgrounds was a special source of concern since these pupils might project cues that would make it easy for teachers to underestimate their potential.

The original *Pygmalion* research was meticulously examined and hotly debated by the research community. It also spawned an incredible amount of replication and related research. This book (1) attempts to synthesize the decade of research and debate, (2) strives to explain the important components of expectation communication through a social-psychological analysis, and (3) presents the most thorough study of expectation communication conducted since the original *Pygmalion* research and follow-up research by Brophy and Good (1974).

The Expectation Communication Model presented in this book (1) begins with the teachers' expectations for students, (2) examines how these expectations influence other teacher cognitions, (3) charts how these beliefs influence teachers' overt behavior toward students, and (4) details how students' self-concepts reflect differential teacher behavior.

The concepts used to explain the expectation communication process are intended to demystify expectation phenomenon. This is accomplished by viewing teacher expectations as one form of cognition underlying more general social interaction processes. The authors have thus relied heavily on basic social-psychological theory to direct their thinking about how the expectation communication process might proceed. The reader will find frequent reference to attribution theory, learned helplessness theory, and self-efficacy notions. These conceptualizations are presently widely used by social psychologists.

In addition to helping unravel teacher expectation effects, the authors think this research makes several other important contributions. Two contributions that merit attention are (1) an application of a data-analysis technique that deals with the issue of unit of analysis and the interdependence of student responses in the classroom and (2) an attempt to test several social-psychological concepts in a field setting. The methodological strategy utilized and the integration of concepts such as attribution, locus of control, and self-efficacy into educational research will allow the book to appeal to a larger audience of researchers than those interested mainly in teacher expectation effects.

The chapters in the book have been divided into three sections. The first section contains three chapters which present a theoretical and methodological overview of the study. Chapter 1 addresses (1) concept definitions, (2) the issue of whether or not expectation effects exist, and (3) the theoretical model for how such expectations might be communicated. Chapter 2 contains a detailed description of the teachers and students who participated in the study and the classroom observation system. Chapter 2 will be of major interest to those considering replication or related research. Chapter 3 contains the data-analysis system. The system with its underlying assumptions is carefully explicated because it represents a novel approach for studying classroom-expectation effects.

Chapters 4 to 8 contain the collected evidence bearing on the model's validity. The chapters are sequenced to parallel the theoretical model. Chapter 4 contains results on the relations between patterns of teacher-student interactions and teacher expectations, student gender, grade, and time of school year. These results are systematic replications of previous research and they demonstrate the generality of past research to the present sample of teachers and students. In Chapter 5 the notion of teacher perceptions of control is introduced and its relation to expectations and to classroom behaviors is examined. Chapter 6 looks at teachers' causal attributions for the successes and failures of students in their classes and the relation of these attributions to teacher use of praise and criticism. Chapter 7 examines student perceptions of how frequently different types of interactions with teachers occur and how congruent these student perceptions are with analogous teacher perceptions and the observers' coded frequencies of interaction. Chapter 8 examines student perceptions of self-efficacy, or the degree to which students feel that strong effort produces positive academic outcomes. These self-efficacy beliefs are related to teacher expectations and to observed and perceived classroom interaction frequencies.

Chapter 9 summarizes conclusions drawn from the present investigation. It reexamines the theoretical model presented in the first chapter in light of obtained data. Several revisions in the model are presented in order to make it more suitable for describing classroom-interaction patterns and directions for future research are suggested.

Acknowledgments

The research reported in this volume was made possible through a grant from the Division of Social and Developmental Psychology of the National Science Foundation (BNS78-08834). While the National Science Foundation does not endorse any of the positions taken in this book, the research could not have been conducted without their financial assistance. The Graduate School and Center for Research in Social Behavior at the University of Missouri–Columbia also provided important resources.

Several of the chapters in this book are based on articles which appeared in journals published by the American Educational Research Association and the American Psychological Association. The authors gratefully acknowledge their permission to reproduce significant portions of these articles as part of this larger work. The last half of Chapter 1 draws heavily on an article that originally appeared in the American Educational Research Association's *The Review of Educational Research*. The manuscript, by Harris Cooper, was titled "Pygmalion Grows Up: A Model for Teacher Expectation Communication and Performance Influence" (1979, *49*, 389–410). The results of Chapter 4 originally appeared in the American Psychological Association's *Journal of Educational Psychology*. The original article, by Thomas Good, Harris Copper, and Sherry Blakey, was entitled "Classroom Interactions as a Function of Teacher Expectations, Student Sex and Time of Year" (1980, *72*, 378–386). The first two studies of Chapter 5 originally appeared in the American Educational Research Association's the *American Educational Research Journal*. The original article, by Harris Cooper, Jerry Burger, and George Seymour, was entitled "Classroom Context and Student Ability as Influences on Teacher Perceptions of Classroom Control" (1979, *16*, 189–196). The methods and results sections of Studies I and II in Chapter 5 are nearly identical to those in the originally published article. The introductions and discussions of Chapter 5's Studies I and II are more detailed than those in the original publication. Studies III and IV of Chapter 5 were originally published in the American Psychological Association's *Journal of Educational Psychology*. The original article, by Harris Cooper, Gail Hinkel, and Thomas Good, was entitled "Teachers' Beliefs About Interaction Control and Their Observed Behavioral Correlates" (1980, 72, 345–354). Again, the methods and results are nearly identical to the originally published studies but the introductions and discussions have been reworked. Finally, Studies I, II, and III of Chapter 6 originally appeared in the American Educational Research Association's the *American Educational Research Journal.* The original article by Harris Cooper and Jerry Burger, was entitled "How Teachers Explain Students' Academic Performance: A Categorization of Free Response Academic Attributions" (1980, 17, 95–100). The methods and results sections of Studies I, II, and III in Chapter 7 are nearly identical to the published article, but the introductions and discussions have been expanded considerably.

The reported research was obviously not the work of only two individuals. Numerous people played significant roles in the research and deserve as much credit as the two primary authors. We would like to publicly thank and express our gratitude to the following individuals.

Jerry Burger, while a graduate student at the University of Missouri – Columbia, served as joint author for several of the articles cited above. He also performed admirably as a classroom coder, instrument developer, and computer operator. Jerry is presently an assistant professor of psychology at Wake Forest University.

Gail Hinkel, while serving as a senior research technician at the Center for Research in Social Behavior, coauthored one of the original papers, handled a considerable amount of coding of classroom data, administered questionnaires and tests, and performed admirably as language editor of the present volume. Gail is presently managing editor of the *Elementary School Journal.*

Sherry Blakey, while a research technician at the Center for Research in Social Behavior, jointly authored an original paper and served as a classroom coder and data transcriber. Sherry is presently in the graduate program in psychology at the University of Connecticut.

John Sterling and Maureen Findley, while graduate students at the University of Missouri–Columbia, served as classroom coders and computer operators. George Seymour, now an assistant professor at the University of California-Northridge, was a joint author of one of the early papers.

Bruce Biddle, professor of psychology and sociology at the University of Missouri–Columbia, was third author on a manuscript which was never published but which became Chapter 3 of the present book (Cooper, H. M., Good, T. L., and Biddle, B. *Analytic Level Specification*, Center for Research in Social Behavior, Technical Report 198, University of Missouri, Columbia, 1979).

Janice Sato was instrumental in carrying out the mechanics of publication. She helped edit and type the manuscript, and developed the author index and the reference list. In preparing the manuscript, Janice was willing to tolerate poor handwriting and cheerfully helped us with countless tasks.

Finally, we most certainly acknowledge the assistance and cooperation of the administrators, principals, teachers, parents, and pupils of the participating school district. Without their openness toward exploration this study would simply have remained an untested idea.

To Samuel, Fay, and Faye

Part I

Theoretical and Methodological Overview

1

Classroom Expectations: Definitions, Past Research, and the Research Model

Chapter Overview

The relations between teacher expectations, teacher behavior, and student performance have been, and continue to be, active research areas. This chapter begins with a discussion of why expectation research is important. Then, a working definition of teacher performance expectations is presented, along with definitions of the *self fulfilling prophecy*, which serves to change student performance, and the *sustaining expectation effect*, which serves to inhibit change in student performance.

With the definitions in hand, empirical research on the correlates of teacher expectations is reviewed. Major emphasis is placed on studies conducted in naturalistic classrooms rather than in experimentally manipulated situations. The review highlights the work of Brophy and Good (1974) and Rosenthal (1974). Both efforts concluded that in some classrooms high- and low-expectation students were treated differently with regard to teaching inputs, outputs, climate, and feedback. Finally, a heuristic model originally presented by Cooper (1979) is summarized. Cooper's Expectation Communication Model integrated the teacher expectation literature with several social-psychological theories, including the notions of causal attribution, learned helplessness, and self-efficacy. This model serves as the framework for guiding the data collection and analysis in the chapters that follow.

Teacher Expectation Research

Teacher expectations and their possible effects upon student behavior and upon achievement have been salient research areas for the past two decades. In the 1970s, four reviews of expectation literature appeared in the

3

Review of Educational Research (Braun, 1976; Cooper, 1979; Dusek, 1975; West and Anderson, 1976). Other monograph (e.g., Brophy and Good, 1974) and chapter (e.g., Good, 1980) treatments of the subject have appeared in numerous educational and/or social-psychological books. In addition to the standard literature review, there have also been attempts to quantify the literature on teacher expectation effects using meta-analytic techniques (Rosenthal, 1976; Smith, 1980).

Expectation research seems certain to be of active interest in the 1980s as well. The importance of issues such as the mainstreaming of handicapped students and the desegregation of minority students guarantees a continuing analysis of the relations between teacher beliefs and differential instruction. In addition, there is concern at present about teacher efficacy beliefs, or how teachers evaluate themselves and the conditions under which they teach. Finally, the issue of teacher "burnout" (negative psychological reactions to teaching) has recently become a pertinent issue to educators. The study of teacher expectations is central to each of these societal concerns.

Definitions

Performance Expectations. Teacher expectations have been defined in a variety of ways. In this book, expectations will be defined as *inferences that teachers make about the future academic achievement of students* (Good and Brophy, 1980). It should be emphasized that expectations for individual students are not merely a function of perceived ability. Teacher beliefs about the alterability of student attitudes, the students' potential for benefiting from instruction, and the match between subject matter and learner also influence expectations. Teachers have more general expectations as well. These expectations relate to their class as a whole, the subject matter, student socialization, and classroom management. All these more general expectations are *potentially* related to the expectations concerning future performance that teachers hold about specific students.

Teachers also develop different types of expectations for individual students. For example, Biddle (1979) notes that teachers hold expectations that can be characterized as beliefs, norms, or preferences. The teacher who says, "Frank is a low achiever" is expressing a belief. The teacher who says, "I should spend more time interacting with Sally, a low achiever, because she needs more help" is expressing a normative expectation. Finally, the teacher who says, "I like teaching John, a low achiever" is expressing a preference. In this book, expectations are treated as belief statements, not norms or preferences, although these are also important dimensions of expectations.

Self-Fulfilling Prophecies.   One particular relation between expectations and behavior is called a self-fulfilling prophecy (Darley and Fazio, 1980; Merton, 1948). A self-fulfilling prophecy occurs when "a false definition of the situation evok(es) a new behavior which makes the originally false conception come true" (Merton, 1957, p. 423). Thomas and Thomas (1928) wrote, "If men define situations as real, they are real in their consequences." Once an expectation is held, an individual tends to act in ways that are consistent with the belief and eventually his or her actions may cause the expectation to become reality.

Consider the case of a first-grade teacher who feels that a child should be placed in a special-education classroom. Because of this belief, the teacher refers the child to the school psychologist to interview and test. If the school psychologist agrees with the teacher and interprets the child's performance as warranting special education, have we witnessed a self-fulfilling prophecy? The answer is no, if the child truly meets the criteria for special placement. A self-fulfilling prophecy entails the creation of a new response or a new outcome rather than simply a reflection of a veridical preexisting situation.

To illustrate a self-fulfilling prophecy, let's assume the initial result of testing suggests that the best placement for the first grader is in the regular classroom. The teacher, however, persists in the belief that the child should be in a special class and asks for another test. Between testings, the teacher ignores the student's questions, severely reprimands the student for marginal performance, and generally discourages the student's attempts at learning. The second battery of tests then suggests that placement in a special-education program would be appropriate. Here, a belief affects a teacher's behavior and subsequently affects the student's behavior as well. If we assume that the child initially had at least minimum skills for benefiting from regular instruction, then a self-fulfilling prophecy has occurred.

Sustaining Expectation Effects.   Self-fulfilling prophecies are the most dramatic form of teacher-expectation effects. This is because they involve observable *changes* in student behavior and/or placement. However, expectation effects can be more subtle but still have major implications for student performance. For example, upon placement in the special class, our first grader might experience some relief from the hostile interactions with the former classroom teacher. As a consequence, he/she might show more interest in trying to learn. The special-class teacher, however, might interpret the student's interest in academics as temporary and might fail to actively reconsider the validity of the special placement. Failure to respond to such potential would represent an expectation effect that sustains performance or prevents performance from changing.

This situation does not fit the traditional definition of a self-fulfilling prophecy because it is not clear if the special-class teacher's expectations are false or if the student's behavior ever changed. Expectation effects of this form would seem extremely important to understand, however. We refer to this form of expectation effect as a *sustaining expectation effect*. Sustaining expectation effects occur when teachers respond on the basis of their existing expectations for students rather than to changes in student performance caused by sources other than the teacher. More generally, Salomon (1981) writes, "self-sustaining (expectations) reinforce and maintain already *existing behaviors* . . . at the expense of other behaviors. The latter are either ignored, attributed to fleeting situational factors, or considered irrelevant."

In sum, self-fulfilling prophecies *create* change in student performance, while sustaining expectation effects *prevent* change in student performance. Self-fulfilling prophecies are visible and dramatic but may infrequently occur in natural classrooms. Sustaining expectation effects are subtle but may occur frequently.

Research on the Expectation-Achievement Link

Although social scientists have long been interested in expectation effects, educational psychologists' interest can probably be traced to two studies.

Kenneth Clark (1963) promoted the examination of teacher performance expectations by claiming that some ghetto children might be the victims of low teacher expectations which eventually became self-fulfilling prophecies. Apparent empirical support for Clark's assertion was offered by Robert Rosenthal and Lenore Jacobson in their book, *Pygmalion in the Classroom*. In this study, teacher expectations were manipulated telling teachers that a test could identify those students who were about to bloom intellectually. Teachers were led to believe certain students would show large achievement gains during the school year. In reality, students were randomly chosen and there was no veridical reason to believe they would show atypical growth. Achievement information at the end of the school year seemed to provide evidence that children described as "bloomers" did better than comparable students who were not given this label. However, the positive results were confined primarily to the first two grades and there was serious question about the interpretability of the achievement test at these grade levels. Also there was considerable controversy (e.g., Claiborn, 1969; Snow, 1969) concerning the completeness of the data that Rosenthal and Jacobson presented. One major issue was whether teachers did in fact treat these students differently from other students. That question was impossible to answer, since classroom behavior was not observed in the *Pygmalion* study.

Experimental Research. The publication of *Pygmalion in the Classroom* stimulated many attempts to manipulate expectations and to relate them to subsequent achievement change. Attempts by other investigators to replicate the initial *Pygmalion* findings, or to illustrate their plausibility using different designs, did not meet with uniform success. Claiborn (1969) found no evidence that teachers treated low-expectation students differently in control and experimental classes, nor did he find that teacher expectations were related to student performance measures. However, there were some studies which did produce results that indicated some support for classroom self-fulfilling prophecies. Meichenbaum, Bowers, and Ross (1969) studied fourteen female adolescent offenders in the classrooms of four teachers who were teaching all the girls. Their results indicated that in comparison with controls girls randomly labeled "late-bloomers" significantly improved their performance on objectively graded tests. However, no differences were found in subjective evaluations, such as student performance on essays.

Research by Schrank (1968, 1970) provides other evidence that expectations which instructors hold about students may affect student performance. These studies also illustrate why some of the attempts to replicate or to secure findings similar to the original *Pygmalion* study may have failed. In an initial study, Schrank (1968) told some instructors that the class they would work with had high learning potential while other instructors were led to believe their class had low learning potential. Actually, there was no factual base for these expectations; the groups had been randomly formed. Still, students of instructors who held high expectations learned more than students of instructors who expected little student learning. In the follow-up experiment, Schrank (1970) simulated the earlier manipulation of teacher expectations. In this study, the teachers actually knew that the students had been grouped by random selection rather than by ability levels. He then asked instructors to teach the groups as if they had been grouped by ability level. Under these conditions, no expectation effects were observed.

Similar results have been found by other investigators. Fleming and Anttonen (1971) tried to falsify IQ information describing children. Teachers simply refused to believe the phony information and as a consequence, the information did not affect their treatment of students. Many studies that failed to produce experimentally induced expectation effects may involve teachers who refuse to believe or forget the expectation information.

Naturalistic Research. In experimental research, investigators try to create expectations, usually by raising teachers' performance expectations for individual students. An alternative methodology for examining teacher-expectation effects is to use naturalistic procedures. Rather than attempting to create or to manipulate teacher expectations, researchers can allow teachers to describe their expectations and then study their consequences for student outcomes. Unfortunately, in most naturalistic studies, investigators have not determined whether teacher expectations are appropriate (accurate) or inappropriate.

McDonald and Elias (1976) used a quasi-experimental technique to explore the relation between teacher expectations and individual students' achievement. At the beginning of the school year, they identified students with similar achievement scores, but for whom teachers had expressed different expectations. The students for whom teachers held high expectations subsequently performed better than did the lows. This conclusion corresponds to that of Sutherland and Goldschmid (1974). They also found that teacher expectations for student performance were related to residualized IQ *change* over a school year. Finally, Brattesani et al. (note 1.1) found that in classrooms in which students perceived more differential teacher behavior toward highs and lows, teacher expectations explained more variation in achievement change than in classrooms where less differentiation was noted by students.

Crano and Mellon (1978) used a cross-lagged panel analysis to examine teacher-expectation effects. On the basis of their sample, these investigators inferred that teacher expectations affected student achievement more than children's performances influenced teacher attitudes. Humphreys and Stubbs (1977) also utilized a cross-lagged panel design, but they reached the *opposite* conclusion about the direction of effect. These contradictions are probably inevitable in quasi-experimental research.

The correlational nature of naturalistic data on teacher expectations has raised a challenge by West and Anderson (1976). They correctly argue that available evidence is just as supportive of the notion that student achievement causes teacher expectations as it is of the notion that expectations cause achievement. We feel (using the quasi-experiments mentioned above as examples) that recent research supports the possibility that both conclusions may be correct. A reciprocal process of mutual influence seems most supportable by the literature. The concern expressed by West and Anderson, however, emphasizes the causal ambiguity which characterizes naturalistic results.

In sum, evidence that manipulated or naturally formed expectations function to alter student achievement (i.e., self-fulfilling prophecies) has been obtained, although not uniformly across studies. The lack of uniformity may be owing to the possibility that self-fulfilling prophecies in classrooms may occur only under restricted sets of circumstances. For instance, self-fulfilling prophecies may occur only at particular times of the year with particular types of teachers who hold inaccurate expectations based on particular kinds of information (e.g., social stereotypes). The existing literature further suggests that teacher-sustaining expectation effects may play an important role in schooling outcomes. This conclusion can be inferred from studies which relate expectations to classroom behavior rather than achievement change. In the next section, we examine several classroom communication patterns which imply that student performance levels, once established, may be difficult to alter.

Research on the Expectation-Behavior Link

Stimulated by the *Pygmalion* findings, a number of investigators interested in the educational implications of teacher-expectation effects conducted research on the classroom communication process. Research conducted by Rist (1970), who studied the same group of children over a 3 year period, provides a good example of the naturalistic approach. He described how the kindergarten teacher, on the basis of her subjective impression (for example, how clean the children were), assigned the children to different ability groups. Then Rist detailed in compelling terms the unequal and presumably unfair treatment that children in the low group received. In subsequent longitudinal work, he reported that students who were placed in the low group in the kindergarten classroom were also in the low group in the first- and second-grade classrooms. Rist also presented strong evidence to suggest that students placed in the low group received less teacher contact and that these students adjusted to school life more poorly than did students placed in the higher groups. However, Rist presented no quantitative performance data to demonstrate objectively that pupils were unfairly assigned or to relate the impact of "misassignment" to student achievement, attitudes, absences, and other dependent measures of potential interest. Even so, Rist provided plausible anecdotal evidence to suggest that teacher beliefs and behaviors sustain student-performance levels.

A good deal of the naturalistic research that examined how teachers interact with students based on performance expectations was influenced by the sequential model developed by Brophy and Good while at the University of Texas. These investigators were interested in (1) how teachers interact with high- and low-expectation students and (2) how teacher behavior affects student behavior.

Steps in the Model.   Because of the magical qualities with which expectation effects were sometimes imbued, Brophy and Good (1970a) wanted to conceptualize the communication process in terms of *observable* behaviors. Their initial model stressed the teacher's role in the process; however, subsequent revisions of the model (Good and Brophy, 1973; Brophy and Good, 1974) paid attention to the student's role as well.

Their model permitted a detailed analysis of the sequential relation beginning with teacher expectations and ending with student performance. The model involved four steps: (1) the teacher develops an expectation predicting specific behavior and achievement for each student; (2) because of these expectations, the teacher behaves differently toward each student; (3) this treatment informs each student about the behavior and achievement expected from him/her and affects the student's self-concept, achievement motivation, and level of aspiration; and finally, (4) if teacher treatment is consistent over time and the student is behaviorally compliant, the student's achievement will come to correspond or remain correspondent with the teacher's belief. High teacher expectations will lead to or sustain student achievement at high levels, while low expectations will diminish or support low student achievement.

The fourth step in the model suggested that students could mediate the effects of teacher expectations. That is, it was assumed that erroneous teacher expectations were not automatically self-fulfilling. Students conceivably could prevent expectations from being fulfilled by behaving in ways that forced teachers to change their original beliefs.

Despite the potential number of questions that could have been raised in research on expectation effects, most research has focused on step 2. In fact, most studies have examined only the differential behaviors (primarily verbal) of teachers and ignored other potential sources of expectation communication (for example, written feedback to students).

Research Findings Based on the Brophy-Good Model. How then have teachers been found to vary their behavior toward high- and low-expectation students? Good and Brophy (1980) report twelve of the more common ways teacher actions covary with expectations:

1. Seating low-expectation students far from the teacher and/or seating them in a group.
2. Paying less attention to lows in academic situations (smiling less often and maintaining less eye contact).
3. Calling on lows less often to answer classroom questions or to make public demonstrations.
4. Waiting less time for lows to answer questions.
5. Not staying with lows in failure situations (i.e., providing fewer clues, asking fewer follow-up questions).
6. Criticizing lows more frequently than highs for incorrect public responses.
7. Praising lows less frequently than highs after successful public responses.
8. Praising lows more frequently than highs for marginal or inadequate public responses.
9. Providing lows with less accurate and less detailed feedback than highs.

10. Failing to provide lows with feedback about their responses as often as highs.
11. Demanding less work and effort from lows than from highs.
12. Interrupting performance of lows more frequently than highs.

An especially important outcome of the research generating the above list is that *not all teachers* treat high- and low-expectation students differently. As noted elsewhere (Brophy and Good, 1974), some teachers behave toward low-expectation students in ways that seemed to be consistent with expectation effects, but other teachers do not. Hence even though teachers will readily describe students as having high and low potential, teacher expectations do not necessarily translate into differential behavior. Moreover, it is not possible to make statements about the inappropriateness of the twelve behaviors presented above, because the studies on which they are based did not usually obtain student-performance data. Finally, it is not suggested that all these differences in teacher treatment are categorical signs of ineffective communication or inadequate teaching.

However, these behavioral differences do strongly suggest the existence of sustaining expectation effects. Although the evidence is indirect, it is difficult to study sustaining expectation effects unless students are carefully followed over time. With few exceptions, research on expectations has been conducted at a single point in time and with either achievement *or* behavioral dependent variables. Seldom have researchers examined process and product simultaneously. (We believe that both sustaining and self-fulfilling prophecies occur in some classrooms but sustaining expectation effects are apt to occur more frequently.)

Meta Analysis of Expectation Research

Rosenthal (1976) examined over 300 studies of the effects of expectations on behavior. Of these, 37 percent reported significant ($p < .05$) results in a direction consistent with an expectation influence on behavior. Such a percentage of significant results strongly suggests that something other than a chance relation was operating. When the review sample was restricted to classroom and nonlaboratory situations, the percentage of studies supporting expectancy effects was virtually the same as the overall percentage (38 percent). Collapsing across studies, Rosenthal found that 340 teachers had participated in investigations which reported individual teacher data. Of these teachers, 70 percent showed results in a direction consistent with expectation effect predictions.

Smith (1980) performed another quantitative review of expectation effects which paid closer attention to the particular behaviors involved. In general, her review suggested that teaching behavior varied in relation to teacher expectations in a reasonably modest way. Particularly evident was the fact that more learning opportunities were provided to pupils for whom teachers had favorable expectations, and there was a tendency for teachers to ignore low-expectation pupils more than high-expectation pupils. Other types of teacher interactions produced more variable results. Teacher expectations were also found to have a modest effect on pupil achievement and affect, but comparably little or no influence on pupil IQ.

Integrating Educational and Social-Psychological Research

A major purpose underlying the efforts reported in this book is the attempt to integrate social-psychological theory and educational expectation research. This effort is consistent with the attempts of others who are trying to bring social-psychological theory into classrooms (McMillan, 1980; Bar-Tal and Saxe, 1978).

Specifically, we saw attribution theory (Weiner et al., 1971) and notions of personal control (Bandura, 1977; Seligman, 1975) as potential ways for providing the explanatory links needed to make the expectation communication process more understandable and testable. Also, by testing these social-psychological perspectives in natural classroom settings it would be possible to determine whether modifications were needed to make the theories generalizable to one relevant context (the classroom).

Some earlier attempts at a formal integration of expectation research can be found. The Brophy and Good (1970a, 1974) sequence of relations noted above is one such attempt. In addition, Rosenthal (1974) suggested four general social dimensions of teacher behavior that might be involved in the sequence. Since our model employs Rosenthal's four dimensions as building blocks, his work will be briefly reviewed below. (For a more complete review of supporting research, see Cooper, 1979; Rosenthal, 1974.)

The Rosenthal (1974) Four-Factor Categorization.   Rosenthal (1974) provided a four-factor typology for summarizing behaviors associated with teacher expectations. The four factors were (1) climate, (2) input, (3) output, and (4) feedback.

First, teachers appear to create a warmer *socioemotional atmosphere* for brighter students. To investigate this possibility, Chaikin, Sigler, and Derlega (1974) videotaped simulated tutorial sessions in order to study nonverbal differences in expectation communication. It was found that teachers who believed they were interacting with high-expectation students smiled and nodded their heads more often than did teachers interacting with low-expectation students. Teachers also leaned toward

highs and looked them in the eyes more frequently. Kester and Letchworth (1972) induced expectations in professional teachers and observed
actual classrooms. They reported that teachers were most supportive and
friendly toward high-expectation students. Thus, it seems that many nonverbal behaviors associated with positive emotional attachment are displayed by teachers most frequently in interactions with students believed
to have more potential.

There is also evidence indicating that teachers' *verbal inputs* to students are dependent on performance expectations. Students labeled low
expectation have been found to receive fewer opportunities to learn new
material than are students labeled high (e.g., Beez, 1970). Lows also have
less difficult material taught to them (e.g., Cornbleth, Davis, and Button,
1974; Jeter and Davis, 1973, as reported in Jeter, 1975). The quantity and
quality of teacher attempts at novel instruction thus seem associated with
expectations.

The third factor, *verbal output,* can be operationally defined as
(1) the frequency with which academic interactions take place, and
(2) the teacher's persistence in pursuing interactions to a satisfactory conclusion. From the student's perspective, output means the number of
times the teacher gives feedback, instruction, or encouragement and the
length of time the teacher is willing to spend on a given contact. With regard to the latter variable, research indicates that teachers tend to stay
with highs longer after they have failed to answer a question (Brophy and
Good, 1970a). This persistence following failure takes the form of more
clue-giving, more repetition, and/or more rephrasing when highs answer a
question incorrectly than when lows answer incorrectly. Teachers have
also been found to pay closer attention to responses of students described
as gifted (Rothbart, Dalfen, and Barrett, 1971). Finally, Rowe (1974)
found that teachers allowed highs longer to respond before redirecting
unanswered questions to other class members.

Among the best researched behavioral correlates of performance expectations is the absolute *frequency of interaction.* Brophy and Good
(1974) cited twenty studies (primarily naturalistic observation) in which
the frequency of teacher-student academic interactions was assessed. Of
these studies, thirteen reported that teachers more often engaged in
academic contacts with high- than low-expectation students. The remaining seven studies reported no total frequency differences. This finding is
even more dramatic when the interaction initiator is taken into account.
Of the seven studies reporting no differences in total interaction frequency, two reported differences when total contacts were broken down into
student- and teacher-initiated contacts (e.g., Brophy and Good, 1970a).

The finding that high-expectation students will seek more academic
contact with the teacher than will low-expectation students is thus strongly supported by these twenty studies. However, teachers may equalize or
accentuate this difference through their own initiation. A substantial

number of studies can be found reporting that teachers initiated more contacts with highs (Good, 1970; Kester and Letchworth, 1972), or more interactions with lows (Evertson et al., note 1.2), or showed no initiation differences at all (Brophy and Good, 1970a; Claiborn, 1969). It seems then that while expectations often influence teacher initiation of contacts, the direction this influence takes follows no general pattern. Rather, the teacher-contact initiative may be a function of teaching strategy differences.

To summarize research concerning the output factor: teachers often show more willingness to pursue an answer with highs than with lows. Furthermore, highs seem to create more output opportunities for themselves, while teachers vary in whether they equalize or accentuate contact frequency differences.

The final factor, *feedback*, involves the teacher's use of praise and criticism after an academic exchange. As with student initiations, Brophy and Good (1974) found a fairly consistent pattern of teacher use of reinforcement. Teachers tended to praise high-expectation students more, and proportionately more per correct response, while lows were criticized more, and proportionately more per incorrect response. This result was based on studies which simply count positive and negative use of affect or which, allowing for the greater opportunity available to be positive toward highs, adjust praise and criticism use by the number of correct and incorrect responses.

The conclusion, in general, held whether the methodology employed used induced expectations (e.g., Meichenbaum et al., 1969) or naturally occurring expectations (e.g., Brophy and Good, 1970a; Dalton, 1969), as long as professional teachers were subjects. Evidence since 1974 remains consistent with this conclusion (e.g., Cooper and Baron, 1977; Firestone and Brody, 1975). The fact that lows tend to receive more criticism and less praise from professional teachers plays a central role in the Expectation Communication Model described below.

For each of the four factors, enough evidence exists to conclude that the phenomenon is real. As with the performance outcome studies cited earlier, however, the appearance of these process differences in specific instances cannot be assumed. For example, Claiborn (1969) found no differences in teacher warmth dependent on expectations, and Jones (1972) found no differences in teacher persistence in seeking responses. Again, it is apparent that teacher variation in susceptibility to expectation effects exists and explanations need to address these differences. In the only study to date which directly tested the four-factor theory (with multiple dependent variables for each factor), Taylor (1979) found support for the input and output factors only. However, this study involved laboratory simulation rather than naturalistic observation. Chapter 4 presents the results of our attempt to replicate these findings.

Evaluating the Consequences of Differential Behavior. It would seem that students who are taught less-difficult material and who are presented with less novel instruction should eventually show correspondingly weaker performance. Borg (1979) has in fact documented this relation. In two studies, he reported sizeable correlations between the amount of time teachers spend on material and how well students eventually do on related tests. This kind of expectation communication does not violate our sensibilities, at least not when the expectation is veridical. While these are genuine expectation phenomena, presenting low-ability students with material as difficult as that offered to highs would undoubtedly create more problems than it would solve (in fact, the model suggested later would predict several problems). Also, pacing the introduction of new material at equal rates for highs and lows would seem similarly undesirable, *if* students perceived as high and low are objectively different in the skills and knowledge they possess. The problem with difficulty and pacing differences is that they may also be prime contributors to sustaining expectation effects (e.g., difficulty and pace remain constant when student potential increases).

For another treatment difference—the reported greater teacher persistence when interacting with highs—the relation to performance also seems clear. A student who is given less time to respond will less often answer correctly. One can question whether it is fair that pupils' prior successes should influence teachers' question-asking behavior. Persistence differences may insulate teacher perceptions from new information. More importantly, low-expectation students may not get as many opportunities to integrate and express their thoughts.

Finally, the remaining differences, in socioemotional climate, student initiations, and feedback, seem wholly undesirable. Beyond promoting a general pattern of inhibition of low's participation, their links to pupil performance differences per se are not immediately clear. Cognitive social theories may allow an understanding of these behavioral differences. The three constructs involved (climate, initiations, and feedback) are well-suited for integration into a model which examines the expectation communication process from a social-reinforcement perspective. Climate and feedback can be viewed as techniques teachers employ to reinforce (positively or negatively) student behaviors, and student initiations of academic exchanges might be expected to be a prime target of such reinforcement.

The purpose of the proposed model then is to integrate the climate, feedback, and initiation variables into a single process culminating in sustained student performance. What is unique to the present effort is that though the model starts with teacher expectations and culminates in student achievement, the intervening cognitive links are drawn from recent social-psychological formulations.

A Social-Psychological Model for Expectation Communication (see Figure 1.1)

Teachers Form Expectations. Variations in student background and ability lead teachers to form differential perceptions of how likely students are to succeed. For instance, Cooper (1979) found that teachers formed expectations based on preobservational information (i.e., standardized tests, comments of previous teachers), and these affected future expectations, even after the student's performance was tested by the teacher. The fact that teacher performance expectations vary is well-established. The point is made here to indicate that even though the model begins with the teacher's expectation, the process involves so much reciprocal causation that it could legitimately be started at any link.

Context and Expectations Influence Teacher Perceptions of Control. Not only do teachers form different perceptions of students, they also distinguish between *classroom interaction contexts*. Classroom contexts refer to the surrounding circumstances in which an interaction occurs. Classroom contexts have many potential dimensional distinctions. One such distinction is the amount of personal control they afford the teacher. This control has at least three interrelated subdimensions: teacher control over interaction content (what the interaction is about), timing (when it occurs), and duration (how long it lasts).

The first classroom context variable with control implications involves the *interaction initiator*. When a teacher personally initiates a contact, the teacher has chosen the topic and student who is to respond. When a student initiates the interaction, the child has chosen the topic (within limits) and has decided that he or she will be involved. Hypothetically, then, the teacher has greatest control over what an interaction will be about (content) and when an interaction will occur (timing) when the teacher is initiator. Duration control may be greater in teacher initiations also, since interaction content should have contact-length implications.

Contexts also differ in their *setting*. Interactions in public are influenced by group needs. In public, the teacher must weigh the needs of any individual against the "group press" created by other class members. Private interactions, on the other hand, afford teachers more flexibility in determining how long a topic can be pursued, because they typically occur when other students are occupied with individual work. Teachers may thus feel that fewer students in a setting implies greater personal control.

Teachers' performance expectations for students have control implications as well. High expectations imply that more topics and perspectives exist for the teacher to choose from (content). Also, high expectations are associated with students who presumably understand topics better and more often respond appropriately. Therefore, teachers prob-

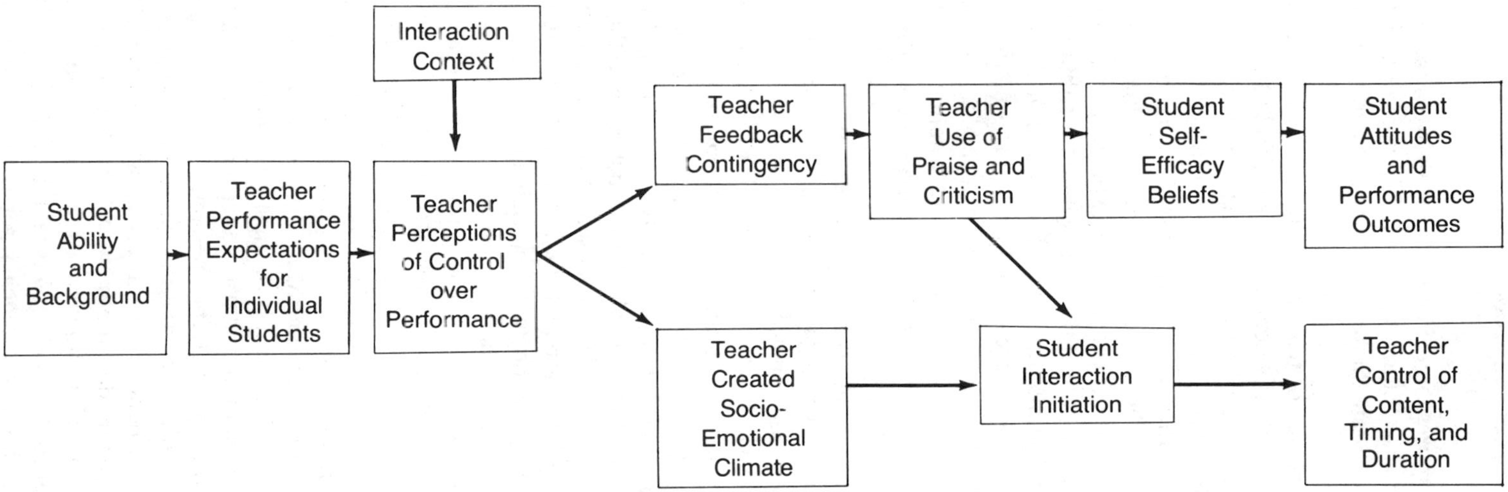

FIGURE 1.1 A Model for Expectation Communication and Behavior Influence

ably perceive more points in contacts with highs where it is appropriate to terminate the discussion (duration). Timing control is more difficult to predict: Lows create more behavior problems, but highs initiate more academic contacts.

The importance of teacher control in the expectation communication process becomes clear when control and likely success are related. Specifically, it is suggested that high-expectation students retain a high likelihood of success, regardless of teacher interactional control. Low student success, on the other hand, may be seen as more dependent on the material involved, on the amount of time available, and/or on the basis of whether the teacher is prepared to expend the energy demanded by the interaction. For instance, the achievement attribution literature indicates that low-ability pupils' success is more often attributed to environmental factors than is highs' success (Cooper and Lowe, 1977). Therefore, the interaction context, with its control implications, is probably seen by the teacher as an important contributor to whether low-expectation interactions end in success. The more control a context affords the teacher who is interacting with a poor student, the greater the likelihood that the teacher can end the interaction positively. When teachers similarly evaluate interactions with high-expectation students, the classroom context should be of less importance.

Relating teacher expectations and classroom-context characteristics to perceptions of control is unique to the present formulation. However, using the concept of control as a cognitive bridge is hardly novel. Much theorizing and research have recently focused on individuals' perceptions concerning their personal ability to manipulate the environment. For example, Bandura (1977) proposed that self-efficacy beliefs influence whether coping behaviors will be initiated, how intense these behaviors will be, and how long they will last. Seligman (1975) argued that a low expectancy of environmental effectiveness is a determinant of depression. Langer and Rodin (1976) reported that inducing increased responsibility beliefs in nursing home patients increased activity and happiness. These are just a few of many conceptually similar efforts; others include deCharms (1968) and Steiner (1970).

The present effort obviously owes a large debt to this literature. The Expectation Communication Model is based on the assumption that the concept of personal control is of substantial importance as an explanation for variation in human behavior. Our theory, however, differs in focus from those cited above. Other personal control theories have been concerned mostly with answering the question, "What are the consequences of believing little personal control is available?" While this question plays some role in our model, the more central control question is, "What interpersonal and environmental circumstances make a teacher's beliefs about personal control more important determinants of teacher behavior?" Since our question about teacher personal control in different classroom settings is unique, the research described in Chapter 5 involves the creation of an instrument for measuring teacher perceptions of control. It examines (1) how student and setting variations affect control perceptions and (2) how teacher perceptions of control relate to classroom behavior.

Teachers' Perceptions of Control Influence Climate and Feedback Contingencies. We have seen that teacher control over low-expectation student performance may vary from context to context and teacher control may be important for lows' success. It seems reasonable to conclude then that some contexts are more desirable than others for interactions with lows, at least from the perspective of some teachers. A teacher can influence the content, timing, and duration of lows' exchanges by using feedback and climate to inhibit interactions in low control settings and to increase high control setting interactions. Specifically, it is hypothesized that *control over lows' performance can be maximized by inhibiting their initiations and seeking lows out in private settings.* Such a strategy might entail the use of simple reinforcement principles. The teacher can decrease student initiation through (1) the creation of an unrewarding socioemotional environment and (2) the relatively infrequent use of praise and freer use of criticism in public interactions with lows.

Teacher use of feedback and classroom climate for control purposes has other implications. A control strategy means high- and low-expectation students may be evaluated using different criteria. High- and low-expectation students exhibiting equal effort on a task may not receive identical feedback. Teachers may tend not to praise strong efforts from lows because praise may reduce future personal control by encouraging initiations. Teachers may tend to be more critical of weak efforts from lows since criticism increases control. In evaluating highs, teachers may dispense praise and criticism with greater dependence on exhibited effort, since future control of highs' behavior is not as necessary.

The Expectation Communication Model implies, therefore, that in face-to-face classroom situations, the use of reinforcement as a control device supersedes its use as an indicant of student effort. Reinforcement will be used by some teachers as an aid in *classroom management* until the teacher believes students' behavior will be controllable without it. Only then will reinforcement reflect the contingency prescribed by broader social values, namely, that strong effort is good and weak effort bad. Brophy (1981) also suggested other functional uses of praise in classrooms.

It is hypothesized then that *as performance expectations for students decrease, the use of climate and feedback to control future contexts reduces its contingency on expended student effort.* Put differently, in interactions with low-expectation students, some teachers may give affective feedback dependent (relatively more) on how these evaluations may affect the controllability of future interactions. With high-expectation students, because teacher control of future interactions is not as important, affective feedback will be more frequently based on the specific merits of the performance (i.e., the effort level exhibited).

Feedback and Climate Influence the Rate of Student Interaction Initiation. To be consistent with the differing contingency hypothesis, evidence should indicate that the frequency of praise and criticism and the emotional climate produced by teachers in class are causally linked to rates of student interaction initiation.

A test of the influence of criticism on initiations was conducted by Cooper (1977). In this study, six teachers were asked to stop criticizing students after academic interactions. Classrooms were observed before and after criticism removal, and student initiation frequencies were compared. It was found that highly criticized students sought out the teacher less often than did moderately criticized students before criticism removal. However, after criticism stopped, highly criticized students surpassed moderates in initiations. In another study, Entwisle and Webster (1972) examined the relation of praise to student initiations. They reported that increasing the amount of praise a teacher dispensed led to an increase in frequency of student hand raising.

Regarding the influence of climate, Sarbin and Allen (1968) manipulated reinforcement rates to high and low participators in a seminar setting. Positive reinforcement (close attention, head nodding, expressions of agreement) led low participators to increase contributions. Negative reinforcement (ignoring responses, expressing boredom) led high participators to contribute less.

It is argued then that the climate, feedback, and output factors may all be causally linked. The three factors are systematically integrated if their relation to teacher personal control is taken into account. Negative climate and feedback patterns for low-expectation students decrease these students' initiation rates. Teacher control over when interactions with slow students occur is thus increased. However, the concurrent loss of effort-contingent feedback to lows may have an unwanted detrimental effect.

Feedback Contingencies Influence Student Self-Efficacy Beliefs. Using feedback to increase teacher control of behavior seems to be an understandable teaching strategy. Inhibition of student initiation should not have a direct effect on the quality of student performance. The sustaining of low-expectation student performance is then not viewed as a result of feedback per se but rather as a result of feedback based upon a particular contingency. Again, the concept of personal control provides the conceptual bridge.

For achievement motivation (Atkinson, 1964) to be maintained, it is necessary that students believe they personally influence their academic outcomes. High achievement-motivated students believe that effort produces academic outcomes. As evidence of this, Kukla (1972) asked male subjects differing in achievement motivation to play a digit-guessing game. Successes and failures at the game were randomly determined but instructions were worded so that any cause was possible. It was found that students who were high in achievement motivation believed that their degree of effort and performance outcome covaried. That is, they believed the harder they tried, the more likely they were to succeed. Students low in achievement motivation, on the other hand, perceived less such effort-outcome covariation. No matter how hard they tried, low achievement-motivated students perceived their effort as less able to influence the outcome of their performance. If arguments to this point are valid, such a perception on the part of low-expectation students may be an accurate reflection of their classroom environment. High-expectation students may be criticized when the teacher perceives them as not having tried and may be praised when efforts are strong. Low-expectation students, however, may be praised and criticized more often for reasons independent of their personal efforts, namely, the teacher's desire to control interaction contexts. Greater use of feedback by teachers to control interactions may lead to less belief on the part of students that personal effort can bring about success.

Several studies give direct or indirect support to the link between feedback contingencies and student self-efficacy beliefs. Cooper (1977) reported that students who received the most criticism in class perceived significantly less self-efficacy than did students receiving less criticism. Interestingly, Cooper also found that interaction initiation and self-efficacy beliefs tended to be related: more frequent initiation tended to be associated with greater belief in effort-outcome covariation. In this study it was assumed that more frequent criticism by teachers implied more use of feedback to control interactions. In a study by Kennelly and Kinley (1975), male student perceptions of feedback contingencies were directly assessed. These researchers found that boys who felt their teachers were contingently critical also showed stronger beliefs that they personally controlled their own rewards. However, no relation between contingent praise and personal control beliefs was found. In Chapter 8 we will examine new evidence relating student control perceptions to both perceived and actual classroom behavior frequencies.

Student Self-Efficacy Beliefs Influence Student Performance. To complete the expectation communication and influence process, the effects of perceived noncontingent reinforcement on personal efforts need to be examined.

That noncontingent reinforcement does lead to performance deterioration is well-documented. Most of the research associated with learned helplessness phenomena is relevant here (e.g., Seligman, 1975).

Most closely related is a study by Dweck and Reppucci (1973). These experimenters had two females present block design tasks to forty fifth-grade children. One experimenter always presented designs which could be solved; the other always presented unsolvable ones. When the unsolvable designs were altered to be solvable, a number of students continued to be unable to solve them. This occurred even though the students had previously solved almost identical problems given by the other presenter. Children who showed the largest performance decrement were those who least believed that personal factors were involved in their performance outcome. The belief that ability was the cause of success or failure, rather than effort, was also found more predominant among poor performers.

A lesser belief in self-efficacy is also associated with less task persistence. Andrews and Debus (1978) found that temporal persistence and resistance to extinction were positively related to insufficient effort attributions and negatively related to ability and task attributions, for sixth graders. Riemer (1975) found that successful subjects given internal attributions (ability, effort) reported more positive affect than did successful subjects given external attributions (task difficulty, chance). Lefcourt, Hogg, Struthers and Holmes (1975) manipulated success and failure at an anagram task. These researchers found that failure had more deleterious effects on performance when subjects believed they were unable to personally alter negative circumstances. In sum, it seems that the effects of feeling little personal control, or specifically, little effort-outcome covariation, may be (1) negative affect and attitudes toward tasks presented, (2) less persistence in the face of failure, and (3) a greater incidence of failure.

With the translation of feedback contingencies into student perceptions of self-efficacy, and subsequently into student performance, the explanation of the expectation-influence process is completed. In a cyclical fashion, student performance differences generated in the above manner can be viewed as sustaining low teacher expectations, since these differences become the teacher's "raw data" concerning students. Poor performance and low expectations continue; teacher control over low-expectation interactions is increased through inhibition of lows' initiations.

Some Related Issues

The Teacher's Intention. Two issues related to teacher intentions must be addressed. First, it should not be concluded that the model suggests that teachers avoid low-expectation students. Rather, teachers may be attempting (1) to control when and where interactions occur and (2) to manipulate the content involved. Teachers may want to determine the timing of interactions which will demand large personal efforts, not make their environment free of effort or failure. Second, teachers are probably unaware of systematic differences in feedback contingency choices. Many reactions to students in classrooms are probably spontaneous affective responses to the personal demands and environmental press students create (see Chapter 7).

Identifying Pygmalion-Prone Teachers. It was concluded earlier, that expectation effect seemed to be related to individual differences among teachers. Regrettably, little research has been conducted into what these other individual differences might be. One important study was conducted by Babad (1979). This experimenter identified "high-bias" teachers as those exhibiting the largest discrepancy in ratings of two equated drawings—one attributed to a high-status child and the other attributed to a disadvantaged child. High-bias individuals saw themselves as more reasonable and less emotionally extreme. These characteristics were interpreted by Babad as reflecting a dogmatic personality.

In a later study, Babad, Inbar, and Rosenthal (1982) found few differences in high-biased and no-biased student-teachers through the use of structured personality inventories but were able to find differences in open-ended interviews and classroom observations that indicated more dogmatic orientations in high-biased teachers.

The Expectation Communication Model offers several possible means for identifying teachers most susceptible to expectation effects. On an interpersonal level, teachers with great control needs (perhaps associated with dogmatism) may be more prone to transmitting expectations. Interpersonally, teachers who perceive low expectation student performance as uncontrollable (or more precisely, teachers who perceive low students' initiations as uncontrollable) would be most likely to communicate low expectations. This condition is a function of both teacher and student characteristics.

2

Methodology: Participants, Expectation Measurements, and Observation Procedures

Chapter Overview

Most of the data reported in the chapters that follow was obtained from a single sample of teachers and students. This chapter gives a general description of these primary participants. Samples of teachers and students used to construct the Personal Control Questionnaire (Chapter 5) and the open-ended attribution system (Chapter 6) will be described with the related data.

This chapter also presents a detailed description of the classroom-observation system used in the program of research. The system employed is a slightly revised form of the Brophy-Good Dyadic System (Brophy and Good, 1969). This information includes how observers were trained, when observations occurred, and what academic content was observed, as well as descriptions of the recorded behaviors.

Participants in the Study

Schools.   Students attended five schools in a midwestern city of 90,000 residents. Four elementary schools served largely middle- to upper-middle-class white families. The fifth school served lower-middle to middle-class white ($\frac{2}{3}$) and black ($\frac{1}{3}$) families. The five schools were drawn from a district containing twelve elementary schools. The schools were nominated by the district superintendent. He felt the principals of these schools would be receptive to the project and no other major research projects were being conducted in them. The nonrandom sampling of schools may have caused "better" schools in the district to be overrepresented in the sample. Also, the paucity of black students meant that race as a source or mediator of expectation effects could not be examined.

Teachers.　Seventeen teachers from the five schools participated in the study with one teacher dropping out after the first classroom observation period. The teachers were all volunteers but were paid a $50 honorarium for time spent on the project outside of class. All teachers were female and averaged 8.7 years of teaching experience (SD = 3.9). Seven teachers taught third grade, five taught fourth grade, and five taught fifth grade. It was not possible to determine how many teachers were asked to participate but refused, since the investigators did not make all requests personally.

Students.　In each of the seventeen classrooms, approximately 60 percent of the students' parents agreed to let their children participate. The only data available to compare participating and nonparticipating students indicated that participants had stronger internal locus of control beliefs than did nonparticipants. It is quite likely as well that teachers generally held higher expectations for participants than nonparticipants. This possibility could not be formally assessed because teachers did not provide expectations for nonparticipating students.

From among the pool of consenting students, twelve were chosen from each class for inclusion in the study. The twelve participants in each class were selected by dividing all students in a class into six groups, representing a full crossing of student gender with three levels of teacher expectation (high/average/low). A total of 204 students took part in the project.

Teacher-Expectation Measurement

Teachers were asked to rank all consenting students according to their (1) "probability of success at verbal academic tasks" and (2) "general academic potential." Most teachers exhibited a strong correlation between the two rankings with the average correlation for a teacher being $r = .84$. In fact, some teachers used identical ranking on the two questions. Few teachers asked for the option to list ties.

The average of the two rankings was then calculated for each student. Based on these averages, equal-sized high-, average-, and low-expectation groups were formed *within each class*. Two males and two females were then chosen from each of the three groups.

The measure of teacher expectations contained no assessment of the *accuracy* of teacher beliefs. Teacher expectations were not manipulated nor was the discrepancy gauged between teacher expectations and objective student performance. Therefore, the results of this study probably pertain more to *sustaining expectation effects* than to *self-fulfilling prophecies* (see Chapter 1).

Overview of Data Collection

Data were collected in three phases. During the *fall phase* (September and October, 1978), teachers provided: (1) initial expectation rankings of students; (2) perceptions of their control over interactions with each student; and (3) causal attributions for each student's successes and failures. Students concurrently answered a locus of control questionnaire (the Intellectual Achievement Responsibility Scale, Crandall et al., 1965). Finally, teacher-student classroom interactions were observed. During the *winter phase* (January and February, 1979), the classroom observations were repeated, as were the teacher rankings of student ability and potential and teacher causal attributions for student performance. No data from students was collected in winter. During the *spring phase* (April and May, 1979), teachers provided (1) final rankings of the students, (2) causal attributions, and (3) perceptions of how frequently different types of interactions occurred with different students in their classes. Students provided (1) locus of control perceptions and (2) frequency of interaction perceptions paralleling those provided by teachers. Classroom observations were undertaken for a third time.

The remainder of this chapter describes the classroom-observation system. The cognitive measures are described in the individual chapters relating to their results.

The Classroom-Observation System

The classroom observation system used was a modification of the Teacher-Child Dyadic Interaction Coding System (Brophy and Good, 1969; Good and Brophy, 1970). This system has been used extensively for observation of naturally occurring classroom behavior (e.g., Brophy and Good, 1974). One advantage of the Dyadic System is that it is relatively low inference: it asks observers to code behaviors described in primarily operational terms. Another advantage is that it is easily modifiable to meet the purposes of particular investigations. The present coding system is just such a modification.

In most instances, the modifications were simply the elimination of categories. Categories were eliminated if they were not relevant enough to the Expectation Communication Model to justify their collection in light of their possible adverse effect on the reliability with which more central data could be coded. In some important instances, however, the alterations entailed the creation of new categories or required changes in definitions of previously used categories.

Focus of Observations. The following foci of observations were retained from the original Dyadic Coding System:

1. Only classroom interactions in which the teacher dealt with a single child were coded; expository lecturing and other situations in which the teacher addressed the class as a group were omitted.
2. The teacher's interactions in a class were recorded and summarized separately for each student. Thus, the student or the class could be treated as the unit of analysis; this strategy allowed the study of intraclass individual differences as well as interclass differences (see Chapter 3).

In addition, the following modification of the Dyadic Coding System focus was made:

1. Coding of dyadic interaction took place only when each child in the class had an *equal* chance to take part. Operationally, coding took place only in settings where (*a*) the class as a whole was engaged in the same activity; or (*b*) individual seatwork occurred. Instances in which the class divided into subgroups and the teacher worked with a single group (i.e., reading groups) were *not* coded.

Important Distinctions in Interactions. Four distinctions in interactions, all of which appear in the original coding system, had particular relevance to this modification:

1. *Academic versus nonacademic exchanges.* Rosenthal's (1974) feedback factor pertained to academic exchanges only. Also, when teachers engage students in nonacademic exchanges, like stating rules or reprimanding bad behavior, they are engaged in overt controlling activity. These behaviors certainly affect the classroom climate for the student, so they should also be related to expectation communication.
2. *Public or private setting.* The Expectation Communication Model postulated different teacher control cognitions dependent upon this setting distinction.

3. *Teacher versus student initiations.* The communication model proposed that the frequency of student initiations is the behavior teachers hope to control through their use of reinforcement.
4. *Positive or negative feedback.* The Expectation Communication Model, attribution theory (when the determinants of feedback were at issue), and learned helplessness theory all involve hypotheses about evaluative feedback. The teacher's feedback is the student's prime indicator of success or failure at a task, especially in the early grades involved in this study.

Definitions and Examples of Interaction Categories

First, each teacher-student dyadic interaction was coded according to whether it was academic or nonacademic in content.

Academic Interactions. If the exchange was academic, four aspects of it were coded.

1. *Setting.* If, in the judgment of the coder, the initiator intended for the interaction to be overheard by others, it was coded as *public*; if not, it was coded as *private*. A public setting was typically operationally defined as a classroom group discussion. Private settings included (*a*) evaluating a child's work at the child's desk, (*b*) speaking to a student privately (although a few neighboring students may have overheard the conversation), or (*c*) initiating an interaction away from the mainstream of classroom activity (i.e., coming up to the teacher's desk).
2. *Initiator.* This category pertained to who initiated the interaction —the *teacher* or *student*. To make this determination, the coder first had to determine if the content of a remark was a reaction to previous material or an initiation of new content. If new content was involved, then a new exchange was recorded, with the teacher or student credited with the initiation.
3. *Appropriateness.* This category pertained to (*a*) the degree of correctness of a student's response to a teacher's question or (*b*) the appropriateness of a child's question to the teacher. The student's role in the interaction was deemed either *right/appropriate, partially right/appropriate*, or *wrong/inappropriate*. Degree of correctness or appropriateness was determined by the coder's interpretation of the teacher's perspective, *not* the child's or their own. Indicators of *right/appropriate* exchanges included the following teacher reactions:
   (1) "Yes."

(2) "That is correct."

(3) A head nod or similar nonverbal response that let the child assume that he/she was correct.

Indicators of *partially right/appropriate* answers included:

(1) "That is true, however."

(2) "Well, I suppose you can say that."

(3) "No, that is not quite what I was looking for, but that's a good thought."

Wrong/inappropriate indicators included:

(1) "No."

(2) "How does your question pertain to the class discussion?"

(3) The teacher shaking her/his head or emitting a similar type of nonverbal behavior.

(4) The teacher ignoring the child's response and seeking an answer from another student.

4. *Evaluation.* This category pertained to the evaluation given to the child by the teacher. *Praise* was coded when the teacher responded enthusiastically or warmly to the child's response; *affirms right* was coded when the correctness or appropriateness of the child's response was noted by the teacher, but positive affect was minimal; *no evaluation* (or no feedback) was coded *only* when the child's participation in the interaction was ignored; *negates wrong* was coded when the incorrectness or inappropriateness of the child's response was noted by the teacher or was obvious from the teacher's response; and *criticism* was coded when the child's response was incorrect *and* the teacher reacted with negative emotion or disapproval of the child's response. Examples of *praise* evaluation included:

(1) "Good."

(2) "Yes, you really know your material."

(3) "Good thinking!"

(4) Any response delivered by the teacher with obvious warmth or excitement.

Affirms right evaluations included:

(1) "Yes," "Okay," "Um-humm," "Right."

(2) Teacher head nodding.

(3) Simple repetition of the child's response to confirm its correctness.

No evaluation was recorded when a student responded to a question but the teacher ignored the response. Negative affect was usually associated with no evaluation.

Negates wrong evaluations included:

(1) "No," "That's wrong," "I don't think so," "Uh-uh."

(2) "I believe you are getting off the subject."

(3) Teacher head shaking.
(4) Repetition of the student's response delivered in a questioning tone by the teacher.

Finally, *criticism evaluations* included:
(1) "No!"
(2) "Are you with us?"
(3) "You should have been able to get that one right."
(4) Any response delivered by the teacher with obvious disapproval or anger.

In order to create the academic exchange categories, the following modifications in the original Dyadic Coding System were made:

1. Response opportunities, recitations, and work-related contacts were coded under a single category, distinguished solely by whether these dyadic interactions were *public* or *private* (e.g., Brophy and Good, 1969, pp. 39–40).
2. The four types of response opportunities distinguished by Brophy and Good (1969, pp. 10–14) were not differentiated in the present coding system but were instead all coded as *teacher-public* interactions.
3. The four levels of questions (process, product, choice, and self-reference) posed by the teacher (Brophy and Good, 1969, pp. 15–18) were all identified as academic questions.
4. The four categories for the child's response (correct, partially correct, incorrect, and no response) were differentially coded, with the exception that a no response was treated as an incorrect response (e.g., Brophy and Good, 1969, pp. 19–20).
5. With regard to the teacher's feedback reactions (e.g., Brophy and Good, 1969, pp. 19–31):
   a. Praise was coded when teacher praise occurred alone, or when teacher praise followed affirmation of a correct academic response (Brophy and Good, 1969, pp. 19–20);
   b. The category of no feedback was coded *only* when a child's response was ignored (p. 24);
   c. The remaining categories of affirms right, negates wrong, and criticism were coded identically to Brophy and Good (1969), with the exception that only one teacher feedback category was delineated per interaction (pp. 23–24);
6. When a teacher asked a student to answer a question which was first posed to another student, an incorrect response was coded for the first child (p. 27);
7. Call outs were coded only when the teacher responded to the child calling out (p. 27);

8. Repeats question was not coded in the present coding system (pp. 27–28).

Nonacademic Interactions. If an exchange was coded as nonacademic, it was placed into one of two categories:

1. *Procedural contacts* were coded similarly to Brophy and Good (1969), pp. 42–44; 92). Procedural contacts included requests for supplies, statements about classroom rules, and help with clothing or lunch money, to name a few examples. The only other coding distinction in procedural contacts was whether it was *teacher-* or *child-initiated.*
2. *Behavioral contacts* initiated by the teacher were coded similarly to Brophy and Good (1969, pp. 45–46; 74–75; 92), although only interactions resulting in *negative* affect were coded.

General Coding Rules

Certain general coding rules and conventions were established for guidance in ambiguous situations. These basic conventions were as follows:

1. Nothing was coded when the coder was not sure which target student was interacting with the teacher.
2. The teacher's intent or apparent intent was the single most important determinant of proper coding when more than one category might apply.
3. Events that were difficult to hear or see were coded as completely as possible. In other words, it was best to partially code an interaction rather than not code the interaction at all.

Any problems that occurred for the coder were written down and discussed with the principal investigators.

The remaining validity conventions discussed by Brophy and Good (1969, pp. 48–53) were not applicable in the present coding system.

Observer Reliability

The four classroom observers were masters level graduate students who were kept blind to all data on students (though it was not long before coders formulated hypotheses about which students were in each expectation group).

Observer reliability was assessed using three separate methods:

1. Written transcripts of classroom interactions were coded. The transcripts were taken from the passages at the beginning of the chapters in Dunkin and Biddle's *The Study of Teaching* (1974). Transcripts gauged the similarity of definitions used by coders. For this assessment, Cohen's Kappa was computed.
2. Videotapes of classroom interactions were viewed. Videotapes involved actual classrooms in which the teachers were asked to demonstrate as many of the coding system categories as possible. During training and reliability checks, videotapes were stopped for coding after each interaction or a few interactions. Videotapes also gauged definitional reliability with visual and vocal cues added. Cohen's Kappa was computed.
3. Actual classroom observations were conducted with two coders present. Percentage agreement was used to gauge reliability.

Two indices of agreement were used because certain behaviors occurred quite infrequently in actual classrooms, making the interpretability of Cohen's Kappa suspect (cf. Frick and Semmel, 1978).

In September, before the first observation period, transcript reliability was high, with the average Cohen's Kappa between a coder and the criterion equaling .84. Videotape reliability was also high ($\bar{K} = .85$). September agreed-upon codings in actual classrooms were also quite high (averaging 91 percent) but fell when reevaluated in January (88 percent) and April (74 percent).

Subject Matters Observed. Subject matter covered during observation was typically language arts, social studies, or science. Both seatwork and whole-class discussion were observed. It is regrettable that data were not collected in reading or mathematics, but these subjects were taught to subgroups of children. The amount of time needed for observation and the complexity of data analysis would have been greatly increased.

It would seem reasonable to contend that the sharpest degree of differential teacher behavior toward high- and low-expectation students would occur in reading and math, given that teachers may attribute more importance to those subjects. Indeed, in the present school district students were assigned grades in reading, language, spelling, and mathematics; but in other subjects (i.e., handwriting, science, social studies, and art) students received only checks or no checks. Therefore, behavioral support for the theoretical model in noncore subjects might provide a very rigorous test of the plausibility of the model.

Observation Duration. Each observational session lasted about 45 minutes and most classrooms were always coded by the same observer. Each classroom was observed for an average of 7.2 hours (SD = 1.1 hours) during the months of October and November, 1978; for 9.5 hours (SD = 1 hour) in January and February, 1979; and for 8.4 hours (SD = 1.3 hours) in April and May, 1979. Thus, there were three blocks of observational data available for each class (fall, winter, spring) drawn at distinct times of the school year.

Creation of Behavioral Variables

In order to create scores for each of the twelve students in each class, the frequency of seven interactions was calculated. These were:

1. Teacher-initiated public interactions
2. Student-initiated public interactions
3. Teacher-initiated private interactions
4. Student-initiated private interactions
5. Teacher-initiated procedural interactions
6. Student-initiated procedural interactions
7. Behavioral interventions

In addition, each interaction was coded into two categories of appropriateness:

1. Correct or appropriate
2. Incorrect or inappropriate

Finally, the frequency of the following three types of feedback was calculated for each student:

1. Praise
2. No feedback
3. Criticism

To create the seven frequency of interaction scores for each student, the frequency with which he or she interacted with the teacher in a particular context was divided by the number of hours the child was observed. These per-hour frequencies controlled for differences in classroom-observation lengths and for student absences. A similar adjustment was made in the measures of appropriate and inappropriate responses by the student and in the frequency of the three types of feedback.

To create relative feedback measures, the students' praise per hour was regressed on the students' frequency of appropriate responses per hour *within each classroom separately*, and the residualized praise score was used to define "relative praise per appropriate response." Criticism was similarly adjusted by inappropriate responses, and no feedback was adjusted by total responses. A student's relative feedback score, therefore, represented his or her receiving affect *relative* to other class members and given equal rates of appropriate or inappropriate responding. Thus, each student had three absolute feedback scores and three relative feedback scores.

A separate score for each student on each behavior was created for each time period (fall, winter, spring). Not all behavior scores are used in each of the analyses that follow, so the relevant behaviors will be listed in the separate chapters.

3

Methodology: Data-Analysis Design

Chapter Overview

This chapter presents an in-depth description of the data-analysis technique employed in the chapters that follow. The technique is a departure from tradition and has implications well beyond the study of teacher expectations. In the method, each classroom is conceived as (1) a unitary entity and (2) a common environment for individuals. Relations involving classrooms as unitary entities are gauged by examining variation between whole classrooms. Relations involving classrooms as common environments are gauged by examining variation between individuals' characteristics within separate classrooms.

After a conceptual discussion, the mechanics for analyzing a single sample of data twice, once for each of the two definitions of classrooms, are described. Several variations on the method (used in ensuing chapters) are presented. The technique is then empirically demonstrated on a data set collected in this study. It is found that the relations between teacher expectations and certain classroom behaviors depend heavily on how classrooms are conceptualized. Alternative analytic strategies are discussed and found to be inappropriate. Possible objections to the proposed strategy are reviewed.

Some Conceptual Issues Involved in Analyzing Classroom Data

One characteristic of social variables in schools is that they are usually embedded within a context called "the classroom." Not to recognize the classroom as an influence ignores the fact that pupils' responses are dependent on facets of the common environment in which those responses occur (Petrinovich, 1979).

Cronbach (1976) suggested three reasons why pupil responses in classrooms cannot be viewed as independent of their general setting. First, classrooms differ in the average level of pupil traits they exhibit. This nonrandom sampling of pupils into classrooms has important implications for social analyses. Specifically, it means that the available social stimuli in a given classroom are often more homogeneous than is true of the population (pupils) in the school or school district. The typical American classroom is likely to be limited to pupils of a given age and social class. Cronbach also suggests that pupils within classrooms will be similar to one another because of intended differences in the way classrooms are treated. Such treatments include variations in the textbooks, seating arrangements, and daily schedule. Within this perspective, we can also view differences among teachers as intended treatments. Finally, Cronbach suggested that *unintended* treatments impose homogenization on classrooms. Such unplanned treatments include erratic room temperature, breakdowns in equipment, and ambient noise. Though these influences are not specifically planned, they serve to increase the similarity of pupils in the same classroom.

Cronbach's three categories hardly exhaust the potential sources of variability among and within classrooms. In fact, this listing examines only pressage-type variables (cf. Dunkin and Biddle, 1974). Other contextual variations will emerge as a function of interactive processes present in classrooms. However, Cronbach's scheme does serve to highlight the importance of classroom effects.

Good, Biddle, and Brophy (1975) raised concerns similar to those addressed by Cronbach. They argued that several large-scale attempts to study the effects of schooling on student achievement had ignored teacher and classroom effects. Recently, research has demonstrated that much of the variation in student achievement lies within rather than between schools (Barr and Dreeban, 1977). Hence, there are both compelling logical reasons and empirical data to indicate that classrooms have to be addressed as units if we are to understand the achievement of individual students. However, in conceptualizing and analyzing classroom data, there are at least two alternative units and it is important to distinguish between these two analytic levels.

Distinguishing between Two Classroom Analytic Levels. Some researchers study classrooms as whole groups or as units that have characteristics which exist at the group level of analysis. The defining characteristic of a group-level variable is that *it does not vary for individual pupils of the class,* or that *one value is used to characterize the classroom as a whole.* For instance, the number of pupils in the class is invariant across class members. A teacher's teaching experience also does not vary among pupils in the room. Similarly, a teacher's average expectation for the pupils in a class can be taken to characterize the class as a whole, as can the pupils' average achievement level.

The first column of Table 3.1 presents a list of some group-level variables, distinguished by whether the focus of research interest is the classroom environment, the teacher, or the pupils. It is important to note from Table 3.1 that variables which focus on the psychology of the teacher (i.e., personality, general expectations) are viewed as characterizing the class as a whole, since the variable has only one value for any given pupil.

TABLE 3.1 Examples of Variations at the Whole-Class and Within-Class Levels of Analysis According to Three Foci of Research Interest

Focus of Research Interest	Level of Analysis	
	The Group (or Whole-Class) Level	*The Individual (or Within-Class) Level*
The Environment	Room size Number of pupils Furniture arrangement Daily schedule Curriculum	Physical distances between pupils Visual angles between pupils Physical barriers between pupils
The Teacher	Teaching philosophy and experience Global perceptions of the class Lecturing style and behavior Average expectation for pupils Average behavior toward pupils	Expectation for individual pupils Attitudes toward individual pupils Behaviors toward individual pupils
The Pupils	Average pupil expectation, performance, and behavior Variability in pupil expectation, performance, and behavior Skewness or kurtosis of distribution of pupil expectations, performance, and behavior	Individual pupil expectations Individual pupil performance Individual pupil behaviors

In studying group-level variables, researchers can ask questions such as, "Is teaching philosophy related to the average achievement level of pupils in the class?"; "Is seating arrangement related to length of teaching experience?"; or "Is the average pupil attitude toward school related to class size?" These questions relate one research focus to another. It is also possible, of course, to relate two variables within any of the three re-search foci (i.e., "Does the class' average level of an attitude toward school correlate with the average frequency with which classroom rules are broken?"). All these questions examine relations which exist at the group or *whole-class* level.

While the relations between whole-class variables are important, they do not answer many of the questions psychologists find interesting. As Good and Brophy (1971) have concluded, exclusive attention to whole-class variables ignores the importance of within-class group and individual differences. Also of concern, then, is the examination of individual varia-tion within the classroom. Within-class investigations can be undertaken only when *different values for a variable can be identified for individual pupils within the same classroom.* Column 2 of Table 3.1 presents exam-ples of individual level variables, also categorized according to research focus. Questions examining within-class variables would include, "Does a teacher's attitude toward a particular student (or a student's attitude to-ward the teacher) relate to the way the teacher and student interact?" or "Do two characteristics of a particular student (e.g., achievement motiva-tion and frequency of classroom misbehavior) relate to one another?". These types of questions, examining relations that exist at a *within-class* level, are concerned with the classroom as a setting in which individuals may behave differently.

The questions above relate two variables sharing the same level of analysis. It is also possible to study questions that relate variables from both the group and individual levels (provided that these questions are answered by examining a number of classrooms). For example, "Does the average economic background of class members influence the within-class relations between teacher expectations and behavior?" or "Does the within-class relation between pupil achievement and teacher behavior influence the average achievement level of a class?"

The Importance of Analytic-Level Specification. In exploring classroom variation, investigators have at least two options: (1) to view the class-room as a unit and examine processes that relate global classroom char-acteristics or (2) to view the classroom as a context within which indi-viduals interact. The fact that alternative conceptual levels are available means that for social knowledge to be meaningful, researchers must clear-ly state the perspective to which their result applies.

The importance of distinguishing between analytic levels becomes apparent when the search for relations between social variables is undertaken. As an illustration, it can be shown that variables which have a positive relation when viewed from the whole-class perspective can have a negative relation from the within-class perspective. Assume Teacher A sets aside 15 minutes for discussion of a story which students have been asked to read. Assume further that an assessment of the verbal abilities of pupils in Teacher A's class reveals these abilities are relatively low. Teacher B, on the other hand, allows 5 minutes for discussion and the pupils in the class have relatively high verbal ability. Between classrooms, it might then be found that teachers set aside larger amounts of time for discussion in classes where the average verbal ability of pupils is low. At a whole-class level, discussion time and verbal abilities would be negatively correlated.

It is also possible, however, that Teacher A spends 10 of the 15 minutes discussing the story with the relatively better verbal learners in the class and Teacher B spends 4 of the 5 minutes with the better learners. This might be the case because teachers feel a need to ensure that classroom discussions progress smoothly and successfully. The important point is that the relation between individual student verbal ability and discussion time within both class A and class B would be positive, in contrast to the whole-class relation.

There is no a priori ground for assuming that a relation between social variables which exists at one analytic level also exists at the other analytic level. In fact, it is possible that variables that are found to be related using one perspective are unrelated when the second perspective is employed. Alternatively, measures of the same two social variables can show opposite relations, depending upon which of the two separate definitions is used. Finally, a similar relation between social variables could be found at both analytic levels, but this relation might vary in strength between the levels.

The importance of analytic-level specification can be further underscored by the following illustration. One might suggest from research evidence that if a teacher increases the use of discussion time, a corresponding increase in the verbal abilities of pupils should follow. A crucial element is missing from the recommendation, however. Is it meant that teachers should increase the overall length of discussion time available to each pupil or that a *relative* increase in discussion time for an individual within a class will improve this particular student's relative performance? It is possible that one of these recommendations is beneficial while the other is not. In sum, the whole-class or within-class distinction is needed when we are asked to translate findings into concrete recommendations. Without an appropriate specification of analytic level, recommendations may be irrelevant or have detrimental effects.

A Method for Studying Both Definitions with a Single Data Set

Since it is necessary to identify the definition of the classroom to which a finding applies, is it necessary for the researcher to choose to study one analytic level alone? The answer, of course, is no; a single study can contain multiple variables at both levels. Whole-class variables can have single values or individual-level measurements may be used to generate both group and individual information. However, the variable level must be identified for the resulting conclusions to have clear process referents. Put differently, some whole-class variables are derivable from the basic data employed in within-class analyses. It is possible, therefore, to simultaneously study group- and individual-level relations involving the same variables and using a single set of data. This may be done by viewing whole-class variables as the average of the individual-level measurements for a given class. For example, a teacher's general expectation for the performance of pupils might be defined as the average expectation held for individual pupils in the class. Not only is the simultaneous study of both conceptualizations appealing in and of itself, but when individual-level measurements are involved, other analytic strategies are inappropriate, as we shall see shortly.

The analytic-level specification approach recommended here assumes that at least three pieces of information are available on any single pupil in a class: the classroom the pupil is in, and the pupil's status on the two variables of interest, say X and A. Such a data set exhibits a feature called nesting (Myers, 1979). Nesting is present because each pupil appears at only one level of the classroom variable. It is possible, therefore, to identify two sources of variance in any pupil score: (1) variation associated with the general ("average" or "total") level of the variable in the class and (2) variation due to the pupils' deviations around this general level. These two sources of variance separately measure the whole- and within-classroom level effects. Knowing an average classroom score on X tells us nothing about the deviations around $\bar{X}$ in any given classroom. Similarly, knowing that a relation exists between X and A when classroom averages are considered tells us nothing about how within-classroom deviations in X and A are related. This statistical independence corresponds to the idea that no *a priori* grounds exist for extrapolating a relation from one analytic level to the other.

The Correlational Approach. How, then, do we test the relations at the two levels separately? Examining relations at the whole-classroom level is a straightforward task. First, the classroom average scores on variables X and A are obtained (averages, or means, are generally appropriate because they control for differing numbers of students within classrooms). The classroom averages are then paired and correlated with one another

FIGURE 3.1 A Mathematical Demonstration of How Between- and Within-Classroom Relations are Independently Measured and Subjected to Inference Testing Level of Analysis

Purpose	Between Classrooms	Within Classrooms
	Added separately Student 1 scores X and A Student 2 scores X and A	*Paired observations* Student 1 scores X and A Student 2 scores X and A
Creation of independent measurements (for classroom N)	. . .	. . .
	Student n scores X and A	Student n scores X and A
	Average classroom N scores $\bar{X}$ and $\bar{A}$	Correlation between X and A
	Paired observations Classroom 1 $\bar{X}$ and $\bar{A}$ Classroom 2 $\bar{X}$ and $\bar{A}$	*Added* Classroom 1 Z score for r_{XA} Classroom 2 Z score for r_{XA}
Inference testing (for sample)	. . .	. . .
	Classroom $N\bar{X}$ and $\bar{A}$	Classroom N Z score for r_{XA}
	t-test of r_{XA}	One-sample t test (= $\bar{Z}$/sd $\bar{Z}$)

Note. X, A = variables to be related
$\bar{X}, \bar{A}$ = average variable score for students in a particular classroom
Z score = transformation of the correlation between X and A
n = number of students in a class
N = number of classrooms in the sample

to yield a measure of relationship strength. Figure 3.1 demonstrates how independent whole-classroom measures are created and then related to one another.

Developing a measure of within-classroom relations is a more difficult task. Though other techniques are available (cf. Cooper, in press; Cronbach, 1976; Soar and Soar, Note 3.1), the method illustrated here involves three steps. First, student scores on variables X and A are paired for *each classroom separately*, and the paired measurements are correlated with one another. This correlation gauges the relation between variables X and A within each particular classroom. The *average* correlation within classrooms therefore estimates the relation between variables in the particular sample of classes. Before this relation can be subjected to inference testing, however, the correlation in each classroom must be transformed into a Z- score, because the sampling distribution of a non-zero correlation is not normal (Snedecor and Cochran, 1974, p. 185). Next, the Z- scores can be entered into a one-sample t- test, as one might do with any other set of independent measures. The appropriate t- test is as follows:

$$t = \frac{\bar{Z}n}{\text{sd}_{Zn}/n}$$

where $\bar{Z}n$ = average Z- score for n classrooms in the study
$\quad$ sd_{Zn} = exhibited standard deviation of n Z- scores

The null hypothesis value is set at zero in the formula above so that the observed Z- scores are tested against the alternative that no relation exists in the sampled population. A significant t- statistic means that there is evidence supporting a within-class relation between the two variables, in samples of classrooms like those in the present study. The sign of the average within-class correlation indicates the direction of the $X-A$ relation to be expected and the average correlation's magnitude indicates the relation's average strength. Figure 3.1 also presents the steps involved in gauging within-class relations.

FIGURE 3.2　An Analysis of Variance Approach to Studying Classroom Relations at the Two Analytic Levels

	Unit of Analysis	Students in Class Who Score Highest on X	Students in Class Who Score Lowest on X	
		Mean Score on A	Mean Score on A	
	Classroom 1	$\bar{A}$	$\bar{A}$	
Classrooms which score highest on X	Classroom 2	$\bar{A}$	$\bar{A}$	
	Classroom 3	$\bar{A}$	$\bar{A}$	
	Classroom 4	$\bar{A}$	$\bar{A}$	$\bar{\bar{A}}$
				↑ Between- classroom comparison ↓
	Classroom 5	$\bar{A}$	$\bar{A}$	$\bar{\bar{A}}$
Classrooms which score lowest on X	Classroom 6	$\bar{A}$	$\bar{A}$	
	Classroom 7	$\bar{A}$	$\bar{A}$	
	Classroom 8	$\bar{A}$	$\bar{A}$	

$$\bar{\bar{A}} \leftarrow \text{Within-classroom Comparison} \rightarrow \bar{\bar{A}}$$

An Analysis of Variance Approach. A possible objection to the procedures outlined above might be that correlational analyses yield limited information: only linear effects are tested and interactions between variables cannot be tested. In fact, other techniques for the simultaneous testing of both analytic levels are available (cf., Cronbach, 1976; Soar and Soar, Note 3.1). One such alternative would be the analysis of variance approach suggested by Cooper (in press). Here, classrooms are grouped according to their average level on variable X, which is used as a between-units factor. A within-units factor is created by grouping students within classrooms, relative to one another, on the same X variable. A mixed-model ANOVA, presented in Figure 3.2, is then performed on the dependent variable scores. This strategy allows for (1) the appearance of curvilinear effects (when more than two groups are formed) and (2) the study of interaction (i.e., is the within-classroom relation between X and A different at different average levels of X?). It is also possible to build greater precision into each level of analysis through the addition of other predictor variables, using multifactored ANOVA (or partial correlation). In the chapters that follow, the correlational approach is used with the more exploratory analyses, and ANOVA is used when theoretical statements suggest the presence of multiple or interaction effects.

An Illustration Involving Teacher Expectation Data

It is not surprising to find that various data-analysis strategies have been employed in previous teacher-expectation studies. At least three such strategies can be identified.

First, researchers have ignored the analytic-level distinction entirely and have used unadjusted raw scores as data. Luce and Hoge (1978), for example, measured within-classroom expectations (i.e., teacher rankings) and then related these to classroom behaviors without adjusting for the behavior's average occurrence in the class. Results obtained with this technique have no conceptual referent. In addition, this strategy ignores the classroom as a source of variance known to have a strong impact on how often a behavior occurs.

A second strategy involves studying within-classroom processes only and employing the pupil as the unit of analysis. Cooper (1977) and Brophy and Good (1970b) measured expectations within classrooms and then removed from measured classroom behaviors the variability due to class averages. This strategy will produce results similar to the within-class strategy described above, though it is arguable whether pupil deviations around a classroom mean can be considered to be independent of one another. It is likely that the pupil-as-unit strategy underestimates the alpha level (type 1 error rate) associated with findings. The deficiencies in these two approaches will be more fully examined below, when their conclusions regarding an actual data set are compared with conclusions obtained with the analytic-level specification strategy.

A final approach to data analysis in expectation research has been to employ the measurement of teacher expectations only for entire classrooms (Schrank, 1968). This strategy is perfectly legitimate; however, it addresses only the group level of analysis and may therefore ignore important individual student aspects of expectation phenomena.

The Correlational Approach. The necessity for specifying the level at which a particular expectation-behavior relation operates can be demonstrated. Teachers who participated in the present program of research were asked to rate the "likely success" of twelve pupils in their classes in five situations. Unlike the expectation data described in Chapter 2, these ratings were *not* rankings, but could range from one to six for every pupil in every situation, with six indicating the highest success expectation. These ratings are used in this chapter only for illustrative purposes. The five separate situation ratings were summed to form a single 5- to 30-point scale. The average expectation for pupil success in these classrooms was 24.54 with a standard deviation of 2.21.

Also as described in Chapter 2, each of the 17 classrooms was observed for an average of 7.2 hours (SD = 1.1 hours) in the fall. The teachers' dyadic interactions with each rated pupil were coded. Per-hour frequencies of different teacher-pupil exchanges were calculated for each pupil. Among these interactions were: (1) student-initiated public interactions (meant to be overheard by others); (2) student-initiated private interactions; (3) teacher-initiated public interactions; (4) teacher-initiated private interactions; (5) procedural (rule-stating) interactions by the teacher; and (6) negative behavior interactions.

Table 3.2 presents the six between-classroom correlations between the average teacher expectation for a classroom and the average frequency of the

TABLE 3.2 Relations Between Teacher Expectations and the Frequency of Six Teacher-Student Interactions

Relation Between Teacher Expectation and the Frequency of	Between-Classrooms		Within-Classrooms	
	Correlation	p level	Average Correlation	p level
Student initiations in public	−.09	. . .	+.05	. . .
Student initiations in private	+.25	. . .	−.05	. . .
Teacher initiations in public	−.06	. . .	+.20	.05
Teacher initiations in private	+.11	. . .	−.10	. . .
Teacher procedural interactions	−.02	. . .	−.15	.10
Behavioral interventions	−.05	. . .	−.31	.01

six behaviors. As can be seen, none of the relations approached significance. Only one relation approached a moderate magnitude: higher average classroom expectations were associated with more frequent student question-asking in private ($r = +.25$). In general, however, little relation appeared between the teachers' general expectation for students in their classes and the frequency of these six classroom behaviors.

Table 3.2 also presents the within-classroom average correlation between expectations and behaviors. Two significant relations as well as one trend were found. Students for whom teachers held high expectations, relative to their classmates, were called on more frequently in public by the teacher [$\bar{r} = +.20$, $t(16) = 2.35$, $p < .05$], but were corrected for misconduct less often [$r = -.31$, $t(16) = 3.37$, $p < .01$], and tended to be told rules less often [$\bar{r} = -.15$, $t(16) = 3.37$, $p < .10$]. These relations were found consistently enough across the observed classrooms so that chance could be effectively ruled out as a cause for their occurrence.

Table 3.3 presents the raw data needed to perform the two analyses for the teacher-initiations in public variable. This set of data is presented

TABLE 3.3 Raw Data Associated with the Expectation—Teacher Public-Initiation Analyses at Each Analytic Level

Teacher Number	Between-Classrooms		Within-Classrooms	
	Average Expectation	Average Frequency of Interaction per Hour)	Correlation	Z Score
1	29.6	2.48	−.42	−.45
2	23.4	1.41	−.14	−.14
3	24.6	1.03	.65	.80
4	23.0	3.16	−.21	−.21
5	25.2	1.09	.02	.02
6	27.8	1.00	−.30	−.31
7	25.1	1.27	.34	.35
8	23.7	0.42	.28	.29
9	26.3	2.05	.17	.17
10	22.6	1.08	.66	.79
11	26.2	0.99	−.13	−.13
12	25.5	0.11	.66	.79
13	23.2	2.21	.62	.72
14	25.7	1.40	.03	.03
15	22.7	0.58	.35	.37
16	21.7	1.86	.46	.50
17	21.2	2.22	.39	.41
Mean	24.5	2.43	.20	.23

Note. The correlation between the between-class measure is −.06 (df = 16, n.s.). The standard deviation of within-class Z score is .40 [$t(16) = 2.35$, $p < .05$].

because it nicely demonstrates the analytic-level effect. *Between* classrooms, a slightly negative relation was found: higher average classroom expectations were associated with less teacher public initiation ($r = -.06$). *Within* classrooms, however, the "same" two variables were related positively, and the relation was statistically significant. High-expectation pupils were generally called on in public more frequently were than their lower-expectation classmates [$r = +.20$, $t (16) = 2.35$, $p < .05$]. In classrooms, the inherent controllability of high-expectation pupils might lead the teacher to call on them more frequently in group situations (see Chapter 1). However interpreted, these results demonstrate that opposite relations between the same two variables can be uncovered at different analytic levels.

The ANOVA Approach. Table 3.4 presents the results of analyses of the interaction data when an ANOVA model is employed. To prepare the data for analysis, the average expectation for students in each classroom was first computed. The nine classrooms whose teachers reported relatively low average expectations for their students were designated the *low-classroom-expectation* group; the eight high average expectation classrooms constituted the *high-classroom-expectation* group. Next, within each classroom, students were ranked according to the teacher's individual expectations for them, and a median split was performed. This procedure created a relatively high and relatively low student expectation group. The basic data for each analysis was the average frequency of each type of interaction for the two student groups. Thus, each classroom contributed two repeated measure data points.

Not surprisingly, the one—between and one—within analysis of variance on these data revealed results similar to the correlational procedure. The within-classrooms expectation effect on frequency of procedu-

TABLE 3.4   ANOVA Data Associated With Teacher Expectations and the Frequency of Six Interactions

	Between Classrooms: Classroom Mean Expectation			Within Classrooms: Relative Student Expectation		
	Low	*High*	*p level*	*Low*	*High*	*p level*
Pupil initiation in public	.27	.33	. . .	.35	.32	
Pupil initiation in private	.39	.70	.04	.59	.51	
Teacher initiation in public	1.56	1.47	. . .	1.46	1.60	
Teacher initiation in private	.35	.35	. . .	.38	.34	
Teacher procedural interaction	.56	.39	. . .	.55	.41	.06
Behavioral intervention	.29	.40	. . .	.47	.21	.03

TABLE 3.5 Significant Interaction Effects Revealed by the ANOVA Approach to Analytic-Level Specification

	High Classroom Expectations		Low Classroom Expectations	
	High Student Expectation	Low Student Expectation	High Student Expectation	Low Student Expectation
Teacher initiations in public	1.33	1.62	1.81	1.33
Teacher initiations in private	.36	.34	.31	.42

ral interactions [$F(1, 14) = 4.23, p < .06$] and behavioral interventions [$F(1, 14) = 6.41, p < .03$] were replicated, while the effect on teacher initiations in public fell short of significance. One between-classrooms expectation effect which did not appear in the correlational analysis emerged: students in classrooms for which teachers held relatively high expectations initiated more interactions than did students in low average expectation classrooms [$F(1, 14) = 5.53, p < .04$].

Perhaps most interestingly, the ANOVA approach revealed two interactions between analytic levels. Table 3.5 presents the relevant means. Apparently the relative difference in the frequency of teacher initiations toward high- and low-expectation students within a class "depended on" the teacher's average expectation for the class as a whole. In high-expectation classrooms, the lower-expectation students were called on more in public, whereas in low-expectation classrooms the higher-expectation students received more public initiations [$F(1, 14) = 4.28, p < .06$]. Also, teachers in high-expectation classrooms appeared not to differ in their amount of private question-asking toward highs or lows, while low expectations for the classroom as a whole tended to be associated with more frequent teacher-initiated private interactions with lows than with highs [$F(1, 14) = 3.54, p < .09$].

A Comparison of Analytic Models

It was noted earlier that three other analytic strategies for data of this sort have been used in other investigations. The first strategy, a raw-score analysis, was criticized for not having a clear concept referent. Table 3.6 presents the results of raw score analyses of the present data. The reader can compare the results in Table 3.6 with those in Table 3.2. Note first that in four instances correlational analyses with analytic level specified (Table 3.2) reveal opposite directions for between- and within-classroom relations. The raw-score analyses (Table 3.6) for the two relations involving pupil initiations have signs similar to the between-classroom analytic level, and the two relations involving teacher initiations have signs similar

TABLE 3.6   Results of Expectation-Behavior Analyses Using Two Alternative Analytic
Strategies

	Raw-Score Analysis[1]		Within-Classroom Student as Unit Analysis[2]	
	Correlation	p level	Correlation	p level
Pupil initiations in public	−.02	. . .	+.00	
Pupil initiations in private	+.02	. . .	−.06	
Teacher initiations in public	+.15	.04	+.27	.0002
Teacher initiations in private	−.02	. . .	−.09	
Teacher procedural interactions	−.13	.07	−.22	.003
Behavioral interventions	−.28	.0001	−.35	.0001

[1] The raw score analyses are the bivariate correlations with no adjustment for classroom. df
for *p* level is 203.
[2] The within-classroom analyses are partial correlations, with the effect of classroom controlled out of the data. df for *p* level is 186.

to the correlational within-classroom analysis. This demonstrates that it is
impossible to identify the level at which a raw-score result applies when
the raw-score analysis is the only information available. It is also interesting to note that when different definitions produce opposite relations between variables, raw-score analyses in this study tend to take the sign of
the stronger level effect, but reveal a lesser magnitude.

The second alternative strategy employs a statistical control for between-classroom variance and then uses the pupil as unit of analysis.
When pupils are used as units, however, assumptive errors are made
which inflate type 1 error rates. Specifically, this strategy violates the in-
ference-testing assumption that separate measurements are independent.
Because deviations around a shared mean are used in the pupil-as-unit
approach, we know that if one pupil's score deviates above the mean,
other scores in the same class should deviate below the mean (i.e., any
random pairing of scores should produce a negative correlation). Unfortunately, the independence of observations assumption is the only
assumption underlying inferential tests which needs to be adhered to in a
strict fashion (Lindquist, 1953; Poynor, 1974). If it is violated, the estimate of error from the data may be too small or the degrees of freedom
for error may be too large.

Table 3.6 presents the results of within-classroom analyses of the expectation-behavior data using the pupil as unit (with pupils' raw scores
deviated from their class mean). Again, in comparing Tables 3.2 and 3.6,
it can be seen that the two competing within-classroom analysis strategies
produce identical directions for the bivariate relations. The strategies also
reveal similar estimated magnitudes for relations. What is dissimilar
about the two analyses are their estimated probabilities that true null results

have been falsely rejected. Page (1975) and others have argued that when one uses the pupil as the unit of analysis, inferential probabilities may suggest more confidence in the effect than the data actually warrant.

The final data-analysis strategy involves simply performing the between-classroom analyses. This strategy is inefficient in that it does not use all the information available in the data set. In addition, it ignores the within-classroom process, which may be most crucial in the transmission of expectation effects. Indeed, the present example dramatically demonstrates this possibility.

Before concluding discussion of analytic level, it is important to point out at least two results of our demonstration that may not appear in other studies which distinguish between analytic levels. First, it was noted that expectation-behavior relations proved stronger within classrooms than between classrooms. This will not always be the case. The level at which two variables are more strongly related will depend on the variables involved or the classrooms sampled. For example, in the present study, classrooms were sampled from mostly middle-income neighborhoods. Had lower-income neighborhoods been included as well, stronger between-classroom relations might have emerged, since greater variation might have existed in whole-class expectations and behaviors.

Second, in the present example, the expectation and behavior variables were both continuous in nature. It is also possible to study *naturally occurring groups* of pupils (i.e., sex, race) within the present framework, as long as more than one group is found within each classroom that is sampled. Using gender as an example, males can be coded as zero and females as one. Within-classroom correlations can then be generated using these values. For between-classroom analyses, the "relative gender" of classrooms can be gauged by the percent of males or females included in them.

Some Objections to Using the Classroom as Unit

The empirical demonstration has highlighted the importance of specifying the analytic level at which variables are said to be functioning. Without such specification, data will undoubtedly add confusion to the literature, since conflicting results may mistakenly appear to relate to the same causal system. A lack of level specification also limits the validity of recommendations for educational practice.

It is important to examine a few objections that may be raised to the analytic-level specification model. First, two objections to defining group-level variables as the average of individual scores are possible. It might be claimed that "the whole is different from the sum of the parts," or that a "general classroom expectation" might be different from an "average expectation for the students in a class." This is, of course, a research question in itself. Empirical explorations can reveal the degree of convergence between the two methods for obtaining indicators of whole-class phenomena. If the two approaches produce disparate results, then use of the definition appropriate to a specific research problem is called for. However, it is still important to specify the definitional level of results.

A second objection related to the whole-class variable definition as an average might be that certain social and individual variables are excluded from study. Teacher experience and curriculum choices, for instance, are whole-class variables which cannot be reduced to individual student scores (i.e., they do not vary from one student to another). In fact, these variables are not excluded from study. Rather, they are variables which exist solely at the whole-class level, making a simultaneous analysis of two analytic levels unnecessary.

Another possible objection involves the conservative nature of using classrooms as units. That is, using the classroom as the smallest data unit makes level-specification analyses low in power. In the present example, measurements were obtained on 204 students, yet only 16 degrees of freedom were available for each inference test. There seems little way around this dilemma, however, other than to say that the question ought to be more one of appropriateness than statistical power. Cronbach (1976) takes an exceptionally pessimistic view of the role of inference testing in classroom research:

> The traditional research strategy-pitting substantive hypotheses against a null hypothesis and requiring statistical significance of effects can rarely be used in educational research. Samplings large enough to detect strong but probabilistic effects are likely to be prohibitively costly. [p. 8]

A slightly more hopeful alternative can be suggested. Researchers with small numbers of classrooms might not automatically discard relations which do not reach the $p < .05$ level of significance. With small samples, significance levels above $p < .05$ can sometimes be associated with large amounts of variance explained. This convention will be employed in the analyses that follow, but when it is invoked, it will be clearly labeled as such. Also, since many of the relations in this study were tested at three times of the school year, *similarity of results over all three replications* is examined as an additional source of information on the reliability of findings. Researchers with very small sample sizes (less than eight or 10 classrooms) might be advised to report raw data and interpret it descriptively. As evidence in the literature accumulates, raw data from separate studies can be combined for purposes of inference testing.

As interest in the social psychology of education grows, it becomes increasingly important that researchers employ concepts and methods which will maximize the clarity and utility of their results. This chapter has attempted to demonstrate the importance of analytic-level specification and has provided a useful means for its study. Other researchers have also become aware of this important distinction, and the field is collectively beginning to express a growing awareness of this problem and ways to respond to it (cf. Burstein and Smith, 1978; Corno, 1979).

Concluding Remarks

In this chapter, we have provided a methodology for responding to the problem of analytic specification. Our primary purposes have been (1) to sensitize the reader to this problem and (2) to make it clear how we responded to the issue in the research reported in this book. We have not attempted to present an exhaustive treatment of the problem. The interested reader can find more detailed discussion of this complex topic elsewhere (Burstein, 1980; Burstein and Smith, 1978; Corno, 1979). Data aggregation is a topic about which closure does not presently exist. Researchers and statisticians vary greatly in their advice about how to handle this problem, and the wisdom of particular strategies have to be determined within the context of particular research questions and a given data set.

We have taken a very conservative position. We recognize there may be conditions in which the use of the student as the unit of analysis would be preferable (e.g., when students in a class receive different content). It is also recognized that treating the class as a common experience for all students may at times overestimate the similarity with which students perceive and experience the same events. Given the research issues addressed in this book, however, we feel that our analysis strategy is an appropriate approach to the problem, and it is best to err on the conservative side.

Part II

Social Perceptions and Classroom Behavior

4

Teacher Expectations, Student Gender, and Time of School Year

Chapter Overview

In this chapter, an attempt to replicate the findings of differential teacher behavior toward high- and low-expectation students is described. If such replication could not be demonstrated with the present sample of teachers, then studying the more detailed predictions of the Expectation Communication Model would be problematic. Also, previous findings concerning student gender and teacher behavior were retested. Finally, the general effect of time of school year and the specific possibility that expectation effects increase as the year progresses were tested.

It was found that the present sample of teachers directed more public questions, more absolute praise, and less absolute criticism toward high- than low-expectation students. Interestingly, however, both absolute and relative praise showed diminishing expectation effects as the year progressed. Some gender effects were found but there were fewer than in previous studies. Finally, teachers were found to initiate fewer interactions as the year progressed, but the frequency of student initiations increased.

It is concluded that no evidence for polarization in teacher behavior was found; if anything, teacher behavior appeared to become less differentiated toward highs and lows with time. It is also concluded that the general pattern of more positive and more public teacher behavior toward highs than lows permits the further study of expectation communication with the present sample of teachers.

Replicating Previous Findings

The literature review presented in Chapter 1 indicated that teachers often vary their behavior toward high- and low-expectation students. In this chapter an attempt to replicate some of these earlier findings is described. In particular, the differences in teacher feedback and initiation rates which were central in formulating the Expectation Communication Model were examined. If the present sample of teachers did not exhibit these differences, then a closer examination of the more detailed predictions of the model would be problematic.

The central hypotheses for these analyses, then, were that teachers would:

1. Use more praise with high- than low-expectation students.
2. Use more criticism with lows than highs.
3. Initiate more interactions in public with highs than lows.
4. Initiate more interactions in private with lows than highs.

The first two predictions are based upon the notion that teachers use feedback to inhibit initiations by low-expectation students. The third and fourth predictions assume teachers prefer interactions with lows to take place in the most personally controllable context.

Gender Effects. The behavioral data analyzed in this chapter also allowed for the possible replication of previous findings regarding student gender and classroom interaction patterns. There is ample research evidence to show that teachers often interact differently with boys than with girls (e.g., Bank, Biddle, and Good, 1980). For example, Brophy and Good (1974) reviewed a series of studies indicating that males are consistently found to have more response opportunities and procedural contacts with teachers than are females. Differences in the quality of teacher interactions with boys and girls did not vary as greatly as the quantity of contact. However, there are examples of qualitative differences in the literature as well. Cooper and Baron (1977) found that female high-expectation students were more frequently praised than were any other type of student. In related research, Good, Sikes, and Brophy (1973) found that low-achieving males had relatively negative interaction patterns with teachers, whereas high-achieving males appeared to receive the most favorable form of classroom interaction. It thus appears important to examine student ability along with student sex in predicting classroom interaction patterns.

Time of Year Effects. This study will also provide new evidence about time-of-year effects. A major weakness of previous expectation research was that behavioral data were collected during a restricted time of the academic year. Unfortunately, the point at which data were collected varied from study to study, making it difficult to draw comparisons across studies. In the present effort, data from the same classrooms were collected in three distinct seasons—fall, winter, and spring.

Information about changes in teacher-student interactions over the course of the school year is an important topic per se, but it is particularly relevant to expectation communication. It would be valuable to know if teacher behavior toward highs and lows becomes more or less distinct as the year progresses and if the behaviors of students show similar or dissimilar temporal trends. Of particular interest would be evidence of polarization, i.e., of teacher behavior exhibiting increased expectation effects as the year goes on.

Prior evidence on polarization effects is hard to find. Among the few attempts to examine polarization is a study by Evertson, Brophy, and Good (1972). In this study, only three of nine teachers treated low achievers in ways consistent with expectation effects. Observational data in these three classrooms were examined for polarization, but only one classroom revealed increasing differentiation over time. Three other small follow-up studies (for details, see Brophy and Good, 1974) yielded somewhat similar findings. These results led Brophy and Good (1974) to argue that:

> The polarization hypothesis remains untested to date, because the studies designed to test it did not include enough teachers who showed a pattern of expectation effects. It appears that only a large-scale study, including a large number of teachers and spanning the entire school year, is capable of adequately testing this hypothesis. [p. 110]

The present study provided the possibility of such a test.

Methods

Independent or Predictor Variables. Students were categorized by expectation level (high/average/low) and gender according to the procedures described in Chapter 2. Time of year (fall/winter/spring) was also entered into the analysis, along with all interactions between the three variables.

Behavioral Measures. All fifteen behaviors described in Chapter 2 were used as dependent variables. The observational measures were placed into five separate groups representing different aspects of classroom interaction. These five groups were (1) appropriateness (correct and incorrect student responses); (2) academic instruction (student-initiated public and private interactions, teacher-initiated public and private interactions); (3) nonacademic interaction (teacher-initiated procedural, student-initiated procedural, behavioral); (4) absolute feedback (praise, criticism, no evaluation); and (5) relative feedback (the adjusted measures of praise, criticism, no evaluation).

Data-Analysis Strategy. The ANOVA procedures described in Chapter 3 were employed by conceptualizing the three independent variables as creating a $3 \times 2 \times 3$ factorially repeated measurement on the unit of classroom. The five clusters were used in the initial data analysis so as to minimize experiment wise chance findings. That is, multivariate analyses of variance (MANOVAs) were performed on each cluster before univariate analyses of variance (ANOVAs) were carried out on any individual observational measure. If the MANOVA revealed a significant effect for a particular cluster, then a univariate test of the effect was run for each observational measure in the cluster.

In the present analyses, between-classroom expectation effects were not examined. This was because the expectation measure employed here gauged teacher *perceptions of student potential relative to other classmates.* Thus, the results pertain only to within-class processes. However, the data used in Chapter 3 to illustrate the different analytic techniques addressed some between-classroom expectation behavior relations. These tests generally found no between-class differences.

Results

Wilks' λ, the F value, and the p value for each of the significant multivariate effects were as follows: for appropriateness $\lambda = .415$ [$F(4, 58) = 8.01$, $p < .001$]; for academic instruction $\lambda = .520$ [$F(8, 54) = 2.61, p < .018$]; for nonacademic interaction $\lambda = .562$ [$F(6, 56) = 3.11, p < .011$]; for absolute feedback $\lambda = .518$ [$F(6, 56) = 3.63, p < .005$].

ANOVAs were then performed on the twelve observational measures associated with the four significant MANOVA effects. Of these, seven were found to be significant. These results are summarized in Table 4.1.

High-expectation students created more public interactions with teachers [$p < .0001$] and made more appropriate ($p < .0001$] and fewer

TABLE 4.1 Classroom Behaviors Found Significantly Related to Teacher Expectations

	Level of Expectation				
	High	Average	Low	$F(1,30)$	p
Appropriate responses	2.41	1.93	1.51	25.93	.0001
Inappropriate responses	.507	.665	.687	4.38	.045
Student initiations in public	.514	.446	.304	7.44	.011
Teacher initiations in public	1.92	1.67	1.33	17.41	.0002
Behavioral interventions	.234	.234	.416	11.14	.003
Absolute praise	.326	.199	.185	17.70	.0002
Absolute criticism	.023	.039	.063	5.32	.029

Note. F values are for linear expectation effects. No curvilinear effects proved significant.

inappropriate responses than did low-expectation students [$p < .045$]. Furthermore, teachers addressed more public remarks [$p < .0002$] and absolute praise [$p < .0002$] to high-expectation than to low-expectation students. In contrast, teachers were observed to criticize more academic responses [$p < .029$] and to reprimand more behavior [$p < .003$] of low-than high-expectation students.

Gender Effects. The MANOVA results for the gender main effect revealed two observational clusters with significantly different centroids: for academic instruction $\lambda = .215$ [$F (4, 12) = 10.94, p < .001$]; for non-academic instruction $\lambda = .428$ [$F (3, 13) = 5.79, p < .01$]. In subsequent analyses, two of the seven ANOVAs proved to be significant. In particular, it was found that girls privately approached teachers more frequently than did boys [girls $M = .64$, boys $M = .42$; $F (1, 15) = 21.71, p < .001$] and that teachers provided behavioral feedback about misconduct more frequently to boys than to girls [girls $M = .21$, boys $M = .42$; $F (1, 15) = 11.70, p <. 004$].

Time-of-Year Effects. Two of the multivariate centroids for the main effect of time of school year were found to be significant: for appropriateness $\lambda = .712$ [$F (4, 56) = 2.59, p < .047$]; for academic instruction $\lambda = .568$ [$F (8, 52) = 2.12, p < .05$]. However, only two of the nine ANOVAs associated with these clusters produced significant effects. In particular, it was found that teachers decreased their private interactions with students as the year progressed [fall $M = .36$, winter $M = .28$, spring $M = .19$; linear effect $F (1, 30) = 5.62, p < .025$], while the frequency of student-initiated academic interactions in public increased as the year progressed [fall $M = .31$, winter $M = .49$, spring $M = .47$; linear effect $F (1, 30) = 7.49, p < .011$]. Hence, teachers appeared to become somewhat less active initiators as the year went on, but students seemed to become more active initiators.

Interaction Effects. The time-of-year × level-of-expectation interaction proved significant for both the absolute feedback $\lambda = .673$ [$F (12, 148) = 2.00, p < .029$] and residualized feedback $\lambda = .700$ [$F (12, 148) = 1.79, p < .056$] clusters. However, only the univariate ANOVAs involving praise proved significant, as evidenced in Table 4.2. In terms of absolute frequency of praise [$F (4, 58) = 3.21, p < .02$] and praise per correct response [$F (4, 58) = 2.71, p < .04$], it appeared that use of praise decreased for all students over the course of the year but this was especially true for high-expectation students.

A final significant finding involved a gender × expectation interaction. The MANOVA tests revealed a significant effect for the academic instruction cluster, $\lambda = .569$ [$F (8, 54) = 2.20, p < .05$]. Only one univariate test proved significant: teachers had proportionately more of their

TABLE 4.2 Classroom Behaviors Found Significantly Related to Teacher Expectations in Interaction with Time of School Year

| Behavior | Time of Year | *Level of Expectation* | | |
		High	Average	Low
Absolute praise	Fall	.44	.23	.21
	Winter	.32	.20	.18
	Spring	.22	.17	.17
Relative praise	Fall	+.14	+.00	+.03
	Winter	+.01	-.04	-.01
	Spring	-.06	-.05	-.02

private interactions with low-expectation students, especially with low-expectation girls [$F (2, 30) = 6.20$, $p < .006$]. Table 4.3 displays these means.

TABLE 4.3 Classroom Behaviors Found Significantly Related to Teacher Expectations in Interaction with Student Gender

| Behavior | Gender | *Level of Expectation* | | |
		High	Average	Low
Teacher initiations in Private	Female	.29	.26	1.21
	Male	.24	.25	.43

Discussion

With regard to expectation effects, the results of these analyses are largely consistent with previous naturalistic research. Many previous findings involving praise and criticism usage and frequency of teacher initiation were replicated. Specifically, high-expectation students were given more absolute praise and less absolute criticism than lows. Absolute praise and relative praise produced the predicted relations strongest in fall, with diminishing impact as the year progressed. Also, teachers called on highs more often than lows in public. Thus, except for relative criticism and teacher initiations in private (which produced null findings), the results were as predicted. In fact, it may have been unreasonable to expect all previous findings to be replicated in one sample, since no single differential behavior toward highs and lows is ever a universal finding (Brophy and Good, 1974). The overall evaluation of the behavior observations is thus that the general pattern of teacher behavior was consonant with the Expectation Communication Model, especially early in the school year.

Gender Effects. Differences in teacher behavior toward boys and girls appeared to be minor. In particular, girls initiated significantly more interactions with teachers, whereas boys more frequently misbehaved. These differences are consistent with, although not as extensive as, those identified in previous studies (e.g., Bank et al., 1980; Brophy and Good, 1974; Cooper and Baron, 1977).

It may be that greater differences in gender-related interaction patterns would have been obtained if subject matter had been controlled. For example, Leinhardt et al. (1979) have shown that girls receive more favorable interaction in reading while boys receive more favorable interaction in mathematics. It is also possible that the procedure of orthogonalizing expectations and gender as part of the student selection procedure mitigated gender effects. That is, much of what is called a gender effect may be attributable to differential expectations for boys and girls.

Effect of Time of Year. Teacher-initiated private contacts decreased as the year went on, while student-initiated academic contacts in public increased over time. In combination, these two patterns indicate that the burden of responsibility for initiating contacts shifted as the year progressed. Whether teacher failures to initiate caused student initiating or vice versa cannot be determined from the present data. Whatever its cause, the increasing student initiation should have positive implications for student motivation (e.g., deCharms, 1968; Cooper, 1977).

In sum, then, there was no evidence of polarization in teacher behavior over time. Most differential behavior toward highs and lows remained stable and those that changed moved toward less discriminating behavior. Investigators have seldom examined time-of-year effects upon classroom behavior. Fortunately, there is growing interest in such questions (e.g., Evertson and Veldman, 1981).

A Test for Student Polarization. An additional analysis was performed by identifying teachers who showed the greatest differentiation in their behavior between high- and low-expectation students during the first (fall) data collection. Seven teachers who exhibited a pattern of differential behavior toward highs and lows during the fall observation and seven teachers who did not exhibit the pattern were selected for the follow-up analysis. In picking teachers, four frequencies of behavior were used: (1) teacher-initiated interactions in public; (2) teacher-initiated interactions in private; (3) relative praise rates; and (4) relative criticism rates. Teachers placed into the discriminating-behavior group showed all four of the following interaction patterns: (1) they called upon lows less frequently in public than highs, (2) they interacted with lows more in private than highs, (3) they praised lows less frequently than highs, and (4) they tended to provide lows with more criticism than highs. Teachers in the contrasted group deviated from this pattern on at least two of the variables.

To determine whether this distinction in teacher behavior would be reflected in increasing differences in student behaviors and/or beliefs as the year progressed, repeated-measures analyses of variance were conducted using (1) student-initiation rates and (2) student responses on a locus of control measure (the IAR is discussed in Chapter 8).

The results of these analyses revealed no pattern of polarization in student behavior. Hence, in terms of student classroom behavior and control beliefs, the results suggested that teacher behaviors could be *sustaining* student performance in ways already established rather than changing student beliefs and behavior. This result is consistent with the claim made in Chapter 1.

Summary and Conclusions

The data indicated that teachers interact differently with students depending upon whether the student is perceived as high or low in potential. The interaction differences were generally consistent with those reported previously in the literature, and suggested that high achievers have more favorable interactions with teachers than do low achievers. These results appeared to support the assumption that other aspects of the Expectation Communication Model could be legitimately tested with the present sample of teachers. It is important to reiterate, however, the finding that some teachers' behavior was more consistent than other teachers' with the hypothesized Expectation Communication Model. These major individual differences in the extent to which teachers vary their behavior toward high- and low-expectation students have been observed by others (Brophy and Good, 1974). In the next chapter an attempt will be made to explain variation in teacher behavior by utilizing the construct of personal control.

5

Teacher Perceptions of Control over Students

Chapter Overview

This chapter describes four studies which examined the links between teacher control beliefs and other concepts in the Expectation Communication Model. Studies I through III relate teacher expectations and classroom situations (i.e., whether the interaction was a teacher- or student-initiated exchange in a public or private setting) to control perceptions. As the model predicts, all three studies indicate teachers perceive more control over (1) high- than low-expectation students and (2) teacher- than student-initiated interactions. Study IV, however, finds little support for model predictions relating control perceptions to classroom behavior.

Only one between-class relation emerged: teachers who felt more control over their students also initiated fewer interactions in private. At the within-class level, teachers reported more control over students receiving fewer behavioral interactions. There were also several within-class trends: higher perceived teacher control tended to be associated with: (1) less ignoring of student responses; (2) less student initiation in private; (3) more appropriate responding; and (4) less inappropriate responding. Although all these results were consistent with the model, the lack of relation between control beliefs and praise and criticism raised some important questions about the model and possible revisions.

Personal Control and Expectation Communication

Classroom situations would appear to differ in the amount of personal control that they allow a teacher. Teachers may distinguish between various situations according to how much control each situation affords them. For instance, whether the teacher or student initiates an exchange has control implications. If the teacher asked a question, he or she controlled its content, timing, and duration. If the student initiated the exchange, some control passed to the student. Thus, teachers should feel the greatest personal control over interactions they initiate.

The interaction setting should also influence teacher perceptions of personal control. Interactions in public settings (i.e., meant to be overheard by other students) are assumed to afford teachers less control than private interactions. Long public interactions are likely to produce boredom on the part of some class members. Boredom often leads to disruption, so teachers may feel a need to keep public interactions short and limited. Private interactions, however, afford the teacher greater possible variation in what is discussed and how long the discussion lasts.

In the Expectation Communication Model, the notions of context and control are used to systematize findings relating classroom interaction patterns to teacher cognitions. One general (but not universal) finding of previous research is that teachers use praise more freely following correct responses from high- than low-expectation students (Meichenbaum, Bowers, and Ross, 1969; Medinnus and Unruh, Note 5.1), while criticism more freely follows incorrect responses from lows than highs (Brophy and Good, 1970b; Rubovitz and Maehr, 1971). The relation among performance expectations, interaction contexts, and feedback was first described by Cooper and Baron in 1977:

> Low expectations imply that future interactions with these students are more likely to be unsuccessful and more energy and time consuming. Since interactions initiated by the child are less controllable in both timing and content than teacher-initiated interactions criticism may be dispensed more freely and praise less freely to low expectation students to decrease these students' seeking-out behavior. Thus, by using feedback to discourage unsolicited interactions by low expectation students, teachers may be attempting to . . . [exert] greater control over the content of interactions and their own preparedness for expending energy. [p. 417]

It was also suggested by Cooper and Baron that because control is more often a teacher's purpose when giving low-expectation students feedback, these students may perceive they are less able to control what happens to them in exchanges with the teacher than their high-expectation counterparts (see Chapter 1).

In essence, then, four sets of relations were proposed by Cooper and Baron:

1. Teacher perceptions of control over interaction content and timing correlate positively with teacher expectations for student performance.

2. Teachers perceive greater control over interactions they initiate than over student-initiated interactions.
3. Teacher perception of control over students correlates positively with amount of praising and negatively with amount of criticizing of student work.
4. Initiations of interaction by students correlate positively with the frequency of teacher praise of student work and negatively with criticism of student work.

Two goals were suggested by Cooper and Baron as underlying the teachers' feedback contingencies. These goals were (1) to increase the students' likelihood of experiencing success and (2) to achieve greater personal control over when the teachers themselves would experience successful and unsuccessful attempts at instruction. Cooper (1979) clarified this second motivation by stressing that teachers were not attempting to make their environments failure-free. It was argued that teachers wanted instead to control *when* their own strong efforts and potential failures would occur. It was also suggested that the differential use of feedback might not even represent a conscious teacher decision. Instead, control-feedback relations may appear because of recurring, uncontrollable, and overly demanding interactions with lows.

There is another implication of the personal-control reasoning. It is assumed that the interaction context and the general expectations which a teacher has for student performance combine to influence the teacher's beliefs concerning the likelihood of success for any *specific* performance by that student. However, teachers may think that low-expectation student performance is more situationally dependent than is high-expectation student performance. That is, the interaction context might influence teacher perceptions of likely success more for low- than for high-expectation students. Studies in attribution theory support this contention (e.g., Cooper and Lowe, 1977). High-expectation students may "carry around" with them a high likelihood of success regardless of interaction context. Low-expectation student success, on the other hand, may be thought by teachers to be highly dependent on the content of the material involved, on the timing of the interaction, and/or on the time available to bring about success. This reasoning leads to two further predictions:

5. Teacher predictions about successful learning should vary more across situations for low- than for high-expectation students.
6. Teacher predictions about successful learning and their own personal control should show more correspondence over situations for lows than highs.

In sum, then, teachers may view their control over interactions as an important factor contributing to whether low-expectation students succeed. It is hypothesized that the more control a teacher can exercise in interactions with low-expectation students, the greater the likelihood of success. When interacting with high-expectation students, the control which contextual variations allow the teacher should largely be irrelevant.

Goals of the Present Studies

This chapter presents four studies of the hypothesized control relations. The first two studies were originally reported in Cooper, Burger, and Seymour (1979) and the second pair of studies appeared in Cooper, Hinkel, and Good (1980). Studies I and II involved administrations of the Personal Control Questionnaire (PCQ), which assesses teacher feelings of control in different classroom settings with different students. The PCQ was designed specifically to determine whether teacher control and predictions about successful learning in specific situations are related to (1) expectations held for students and (2) the interaction initiator. Thus, Studies I and II tested hypotheses 1, 2, 5, and 6 described above. Studies I and II involved samples of teachers different from those described in Chapter 2. Study III required yet a third administration of the PCQ, this time to the primary sample of teachers described earlier. Finally, Study IV related responses on the PCQ by the primary sample to some of the observed classroom behaviors which were also detailed in Chapter 2. Study IV tested the third hypothesis, that control perceptions are related to the use of praise and criticism.

A few points concerning the experimental designs of the studies must be made. The Expectation Communication Model specifies that public initiations by low-expectation students are least controllable. In practice, however, a classroom teacher often will ask a question to a group of students and also will ask any students wishing to answer to raise their hands. In this instance, the teacher and students have both done some initiating. The teacher has controlled content, but he or she also believes (or expects) that asking a student with a raised hand to respond will lead to success. Answers requested from students who do not raise their hands should be seen by the teacher as much less likely to be correct. For empirical purposes, then, this distinction between teacher-initiated public interactions with and without a raised hand was retained on the PCQ.

The following studies also assume that three dimensions of control can be identified in teacher judgments: control over the timing, content, and duration of interaction. In Study I, teachers were asked to provide control ratings for timing and content. In Studies II and III all three aspects of control were measured.

Finally, Study I was conducted with a relatively heterogeneous group of teachers. An assessment of some individual differences in control perceptions was therefore possible. Study II, on the other hand, was conducted on a group of teachers drawn from a very circumscribed teaching population (i.e., fourth-grade, departmentalized teachers). Thus, the two studies together ought to give a good indication of the generalizability of findings.

STUDY I.   EXPECTATIONS AND INTERACTION CONTROL

Method

Subjects.   Seventy-eight teachers (approximately 90 percent female) attending an advanced education class at the University of Missouri–Columbia participated in the experiment. Participants who reported teaching at the college level or at both the primary and secondary levels were excluded from the sample on an a priori basis. This left a sample of forty-eight teachers, two of whom were subsequently randomly removed from the sample to simplify the statistical analysis.

Procedure.   In a regular class session, participants were told that the study concerned "teachers, their students, and some specific conditions occurring in classrooms." A booklet which described ten "typical classroom encounters" was distributed (the encounters are described below). The ten encounters were each presented on a separate page and, after the description, teachers were asked to answer three questions. They were also advised that answers on one page should be independent of answers on other pages. The order of the descriptions was randomly determined in each booklet to ensure counterbalancing of practice and/or fatigue effects. The final page of each booklet asked teachers for personal background information such as gender, grade levels taught, years of experience, and location of present school.

Individual Differences.   Responses on the background information page were used to create two distinctions between teachers: grade level taught and years of teaching experience. Median splits were used to define teachers in primary schools (grades K to 5) or secondary schools (grades 6 to 12), and teachers with either little experience (less than 4 years teaching) or much experience (4 to 21 years). Thus, four between-teacher groupings were created with fourteen teachers in each group.

Student Ability.   This variable was constructed by requesting that teachers provide the initials of three students from their most recent class at each of two quality-of-performance levels: *high* and *low*. This information was requested on an instruction page at the beginning of the booklet.

A summary of the instructions follows:

> Students vary in many ways; however, on the following pages we are concerned only with academic ability. Academic ability can be defined as the quality of performance in terms of tests and class exercises with academic content. In your class(es) you undoubtedly have students who are consistently either high or low in academic ability.

Teachers were then asked to list the initials of three high-quality- and three low-quality-performance students. They were informed that "the reason for putting three initials is to ensure that particular characteristics of any one student will not influence your responses. When you answer the questions on the following pages, consider what the three students have in common."

Classroom Situations. Five classroom situations were distinguished:

1. *Teacher-initiated public interaction with a raised hand.* "You are addressing the class as a group. You ask an academic question. A high/low-ability student raises a hand, and you call on this student to answer."

2. *Teacher-initiated public interaction with no raised hand.* "You are addressing the class as a group, and you have just asked an academic question. You call on a high/low-ability student to answer although the student has not raised a hand."

3. *Student-initiated public interaction.* "You are addressing the class as a group. A high/low ability student raises a hand, and you call on this student. The student asks an academic question."

4. *Teacher-initiated private interaction.* "You are working with students in your class on an individual basis. You ask a high/low-ability student to work with you, and then you ask an academic question."

5. *Student-initiated private interaction.* "You are working with students in your class on an individual basis. A high/low-ability student comes up to you and asks you an academic question."

The five situations were presented once each for high- and low-ability students, creating ten ability-by-situation combinations. Thus, the ability (expectation) level and situation factors were within-teacher variables, with each teacher responding to all ten conditions.

Dependent Variables. On each page, three dependent measures were assessed. Feelings concerning personal control over content were obtained from responses to the question, "How much control do you feel you have over the subject matter of this encounter?" Responses could range from (1) no control at all to (6) total control. Perceptions of control over duration of the interaction were assessed by the question, "How much control do you feel you have over how long this encounter will last?" Response alternatives were identical to those used for the content-control question. Finally, a third question assessed expectations for success: "How likely is this interaction to end in success?" The six alternatives ranged from (1) very unlikely to (6) extremely likely.

Analytic Procedure.   For the two control questions, a preliminary analysis was performed using a four-way ($2 \times 2 \times 2 \times 5$) multivariate analysis of variance with two dependent measures (content and duration control). Effects which were found significant then underwent univariate analysis of variance for each dependent measure separately. Multiple-arrayed means for significant ANOVA effects were then tested using Newman-Keuls ordered-means comparisons. The MANOVA procedure tests the general control hypotheses and protects against some chance findings because so many inference tests are conducted. For the likelihood of success measure, a single four-way ANOVA was performed.

In sum, each teacher responded to ten ability-by-situation (2×5) descriptions, with grade level taught and years of experience (2×2) serving as between-teachers factors. As in Chapter 4, then, the ability (expectation) level results pertain only to within-class relations.

Results

Perceptions of Control.   The multivariate analysis of variance revealed three significance effects. The Wilks' Lambda (λ) criteria for student ability (high vs. low) was 0.87, having an associated F value of 3.76 [$df = 2$, 51, $p < .03$]. This indicated that for the two control questions, the multivariate centroid for high-ability students was higher than for low-ability students. Differences were also obtained for the five situations [$\lambda = .89$, $F (8, 414) = 2.99$, $p < .003$], as well as the ability-by-situation interaction [$\lambda = .92$, $F (8, 414) = 2.33$, $p < .02$].

Control-of-Content Measure.   The univariate analysis of teacher perceptions of control over content revealed significant main effects for student ability [$F (1, 52) = 7.61$, $p < .008$] and situation [$F (4, 208) = 5.38$, $p < .0004$]. Table 5.1 presents the related means. Teachers felt more control over content when interacting with high- than with low-ability students and more control in certain situations. The interaction of ability with situation was also significant [$F (4, 208) = 3.27$, $p < .02$]. Newman-Keuls tests revealed that for high-ability students, teachers reported significantly less control over interaction content in the student-initiated exchanges. For low-ability students, less control was reported for the student-

TABLE 5.1   Study I Teachers' Perceptions of Control over Content and Duration for Each Situation and Student Ability

	Control of Content			Control of Duration		
		Student Ability			Student Ability	
Situation	High	Low	Mean	High	Low	Mean
Raised hand	5.02_a	4.57_{bc}	4.79	4.84_a	4.55_{bc}	4.70
Teacher public	4.96_a	4.48_{bcd}	4.72	4.77_{ab}	4.43_c	4.60
Student public	4.43_{cd}	4.30_d	4.37	4.66_{abc}	4.54_{bc}	4.60
Teacher private	5.00_a	4.71_b	4.86	4.80_{ab}	4.66_{abc}	4.73
Student private	4.73_b	4.71_b	4.72	4.69_{ab}	4.69_{ab}	4.69
Means	4.83	4.56		4.75	4.58	

Note. Means not sharing a common subscript differ significantly ($p < .05$) by a Newman-Keuls test.

TABLE 5.2   Study I Teachers' Perceptions of Likelihood of Success for each Situation and Student Ability

	Student Ability		
Situation	High	Low	Mean
Raised hand	5.25_a	4.13_d	4.69
Teacher public	4.66_{bc}	2.96_e	3.81
Student public	5.20_a	4.18_{cd}	4.69
Teacher private	5.25_a	4.29_{bcd}	4.77
Student private	5.21_a	4.63_b	4.92
Means	5.12	4.04	

Note. Means not sharing a common subscript differ significantly ($p < .05$) by a Newman-Keuls test.

initiated public situation than for any private situation, or for the raised-hand instance. Comparisons across ability conditions revealed that teachers felt more content control when they initiated the exchange with high-ability students as compared with low-ability students. Content control did not differ between high- and low-ability students when the student initiated the interaction, although the means had the same relations as the means for teacher-initiated exchanges.

Control-over-Duration Measure.   With regard to teacher perceptions of control over duration, the univariate analyses revealed significant effects for ability [$F (1, 52) = 4.65, p < .04$] and ability by situation [$F (4, 208) = 2.37, p < .06$]. Group means and the Newman-Keuls analysis for interaction results are reported in Table 5.1.

As expected, teachers felt greater duration control when interacting with high- than with low-ability students. Comparisons of means underlying the ability-by-situation effect revealed no differences between the high-expectation encounters. For low-ability students, teachers reported less duration control for the teacher-initiated public situation without a raised hand than for the student-initiated private situation. Across conditions, teachers reported more control over duration when high-ability students responded to teacher-initiated public interactions than when low-ability students responded. This finding held for both voluntary (hand-raised) and nonvoluntary (hand-not-raised) situations.

Likelihood-of-Success Measure. The univariate analysis of the teacher rating for likelihood of success revealed a significant main effect for student ability [$F (1, 52) = 79.85, p < .0001$]; more success was expected with high- than with low-ability students. Situation [$F (4, 208) = 30.39, p < .0001$] and the interaction of ability and situation were also significant [$F (4, 208) = 6.76, p < .0001$], as shown in Table 5.2.

Teacher expectations for success were lowest when directing a public question to a student who had not raised his/her hand. For high-ability students this was the only significantly different situation. For low-ability students, less success was expected by teachers in any public situation than in a student-initiated private situation. When low- and high-ability students were contrasted, the lows were seen as significantly less likely to succeed in *every* situation.

STUDY II.   EXPECTATIONS AND INTERACTION CONTROL REVISITED

Method

Subjects.   Thirty-three teachers, mostly female, were participants. These teachers were teaching fourth grade and had volunteered to participate in a study unrelated to the present effort.

Procedure.   All participants received booklets identical to those used in Study I, except for a single alteration. The question, "How much control do you feel you have over *when* this encounter will occur?" was added to the Study I questions for each situation.

Analytic Procedure.   A preliminary multivariate analysis of variance (2 × 5) was conducted with the three control measures (content, duration, and timing) as dependent variables. Effects found significant using this procedure then underwent univariate analyses of variance for each dependent measure. Means of significant multiple-arrayed effects were then tested with Newman-Keuls ordered comparisons.

Results

Perceptions of Control. The multivariate analysis of variance revealed significant effects for student ability [$\lambda = .65$, $F(3, 30) = 5.18$, $p < .005$] and for situations [$\lambda = .48$, $F(12, 333) = 8.80$, $p < .0001$]. No effect was obtained for the ability-by-situation interaction.

Control Over Content Measure. Univariate tests revealed that teachers reported greater control over subject matter when dealing with high- than with low-ability students [$F(1, 32) = 5.22$, $p < .03$]. A significant main effect for the influence of situation on content control was also found [$F(4, 128) = 9.49$, $p < .0001$]. As Table 5.3 reveals, the greatest control over subject matter was perceived by teachers when they initiated a private interaction or when they called upon a student with a raised hand. Thus, Study II replicated the Study I ability effect and showed a more general initiator effect.

Control of Duration Measure. Univariate tests revealed no statistically significant effects. Means did reveal, however, that greater control of duration was perceived for high-ability than for low-ability students in every situation, and the ability main effect did approach significance [$F(1, 32) = 3.06$, $p < .09$]. Means were also consistent with the Study I finding that for low-ability students more duration control was perceived in a private setting.

TABLE 5.3 Study II Teachers' Perceptions of Control over Content and Timing for Each Situation and Student Ability

	Content			Timing		
	Student Ability			Student Ability		
Situation	*High*	*Low*	*Mean*	*High*	*Low*	*Mean*
Raised hand	4.94	4.50	4.72$_a$	4.56	4.08	4.32$_{ab}$
Teacher public	4.79	4.41	4.60$_b$	5.00	4.85	4.92$_a$
Student public	4.38	4.14	4.26$_b$	4.08	3.58	3.83$_{bc}$
Teacher private	5.00	4.73	4.86$_a$	4.91	4.62	4.76$_a$
Student private	4.06	3.94	4.00$_b$	3.61	3.26	3.44$_c$
Means	4.63	4.34		4.43	4.08	

Note. Means not sharing a common subscript differ significantly ($p < .05$) by a Newman-Keuls test.

TABLE 5.4   Study II Teachers' Perceptions of Likelihood of Success for Each Situation and Student Ability

Situation	Student Ability		Mean
	High	*Low*	*Mean*
Raised hand	5.18_a	3.44_e	4.31
Teacher public	4.41_{bc}	2.76_f	3.58
Student public	4.76_b	3.85_{dc}	4.30
Teacher private	5.09_a	3.82_{de}	4.46
Student private	5.12_a	4.03_{cd}	4.58
Means	4.91	3.58	

Note. Means not sharing a common subscript differ significantly ($p < .05$) by a Newman-Keuls test.

Control of Timing Measures.   Greatest control of timing was reported when dealing with high-ability students [$F (1, 32) = 12.62, p < .002$]. A significant situation effect on timing control was also found [$F (4, 128) = 22.28, p < .0001$]. As seen in Table 5.3, greater control over timing was reported for the teacher-initiated situations.

Likelihood-of-Success Measures.   The means and results of Newman-Keuls comparisons for this item are found in Table 5.4. A significant main effect for ability was revealed [$F (1, 32) = 50.29, p < .0001$]. As in Study I, the likelihood for a successful interaction was seen as greater for high- than for low-ability students in every situation. In addition, there was a significant main effect for situation [$F (4, 128) = 18.11, p < .0001$] and a significant interaction of student ability with situation [$F (4, 128) = 3.25, p < .02$]. An examination of Table 5.4 reveals that success was least likely when the student was called on without a raised hand. Unlike Study I, teachers felt a greater likelihood for success with high-ability students when the interaction was private. As Study I revealed, teachers tended to report a greater chance for success with low-ability students when the *student* initiated the interaction.

Discussion of Studies I and II

Several conclusions about perceptions of control seem warranted, based on the results of Studies I and II. First, as predicted by hypothesis 1, high-expectation student performances were seen as inherently more controllable than low-expectation student performances. This result was found in both studies when subject-matter control was the concern, in one study when duration control was the concern (with consistent means in the other study), and in the one study where timing control was of interest.

Second, the interaction initiator (hypothesis 2) had a reliable influence on perceptions of subject-matter control. In both studies, teacher initiations were seen as affording teachers more control over content and timing (Study II) than did student initiations. Teacher initiations did not affect duration control. Finally, the interaction setting, whether it was public or private, had a fairly specific effect on duration control and no effect in other control domains.

While the context effects, especially setting, were less robust than anticipated, the pattern of influence was consistent with the reasoning set forth in Chapter 1. That is, the close relations found between the interaction initiator and the teacher perception of content and timing control and between the interaction setting and teacher-perceived duration control reflect the reasoning hypothesized in the Expectation Communication Model.

Some Unexpected Findings. The likelihood of success measure and its relation to control provided some unexpected results. As predicted, the measures revealed that lower expectations were associated with lesser success estimates. Contrary to prediction, there was a tendency in both studies for teachers to see the likelihood of success as greater in student than teacher initiations, although this tendency was not significant. This was especially true for low-expectation students. This result contradicts hypothesis 6, which predicted that likely success ratings for lows would closely correspond to control beliefs. Instead, for low-expectation students, situations which provide the least teacher personal control tended to be seen as more likely to succeed. Perhaps initiation behavior *itself* is seen as a strong indication of positive motivation on the part of lows. The teacher belief that success is more likely when such motivation is present seems reasonable. It should be stressed, however, that the positive effect of initiation by lows on success estimates is only a *pattern* in the data and not a reliable finding. Still, in light of the fact that low-expectation student initiations were not seen as least likely to succeed, we have to ask what other motives might be involved in the attempt of some teachers to inhibit these low-control interactions.

Perhaps the most parsimonious explanation might involve highlighting the group nature of classroom interactions. While low-expectation student initiations might have desirable success implications *for a particular student*, their general instructive value for the rest of the class may be poor. Teachers may be thinking: "even though lows' public initiations are more likely to end in success than when I ask the question, the *generally* poor success rate of these contacts, coupled with my personal inability to control their content and timing (so that they are of interest to other students) makes them relatively undesirable."

Speculating that this "group press" plays a larger-than-anticipated role in the expectation communication process does not require alteration in the proposed link between teacher-control perceptions and feedback. Teacher use of control considerations to determine feedback may still be predicted to be greater for lows than highs. Lows' initiations have been found to be relatively uncontrollable, and this undesirable characteristic may outweigh their relatively successful nature. Using feedback to increase control still leads to the conclusion that low-expectation initiations, especially in public, will be inhibited at least by teachers with high or unresolved control needs.

STUDY III. EXPECTATIONS AND INTERACTION CONTROL: ONE MORE TIME

Study III is a replication of the first two studies. Several important differences have to be kept in mind, however. The first is that the participating teachers were those who were described in Chapter 2 and who provided most of the data contained in other chapters. These teachers are also the ones whose classrooms were observed in Study IV. Therefore, the separate Personal Control Questionnaire responses that are analyzed in Study III are the same responses that are related to classroom behavior in Study IV.

A second difference between this and the earlier studies is that in the first two PCQ studies, teachers were asked to nominate three high- and three low-ability students, who were then rated on personal control. In Study III, the teachers were given the names of twelve of their students who were chosen by the investigators. As outlined in Chapter 2, the target students were chosen to represent the two genders and three levels of teacher performance expectation (high/average/low) within their respective classrooms. Also, differences in likelihood of success estimates reported on the PCQ were not scrutinized. However, if the reader is interested in the relation between PCQ-predicted success and classroom behaviors, this data is provided in the example of the analytic-level specification procedures described in Chapter 3. Finally, rather than use Newman-Keuls post-hoc means tests, this study employed planned comparisons, with comparison weights conforming to the earlier stated hypotheses.

Results

A within-subject multivariate analysis of variance was conducted. The multiple dependent variables were control over subject matter, timing, and duration. The experimental factors were student gender, level of expectation, and type of classroom interaction ($2 \times 3 \times 5$).

The MANOVA revealed two significant effects. The multivariate

TABLE 5.5   Study III Teachers' Interaction Control Perceptions for Each Level of Expectation for Students

	Type of Control		
Level of Expectation	*Subject Matter*	*Timing*	*Duration*
High	5.00	4.85	4.90
Average	4.91	4.71	4.84
Low	4.76	4.66	4.77

Note. All three types of control show significant linear expectation effects ($p < .05$) and nonsignificant curvilinear effects.

centroids for expectation level [$\lambda = 9.63$; $F (6, 60) = 2.59$, $p < .03$] and for situation [$\lambda = 0.37$; $F (12, 164) = 6.21$, $p < .0001$] showed differences beyond chance variation. Since these were the only significant multivariate effects, they were the only effects to undergo univariate analysis for the separate control questions.

Regarding expectation levels, all three control questions revealed significant linear effects: as expectation level increased, perceived control of interaction content, timing, and duration increased: for subject matter [$F (1, 32) = 10.63$, $p < .005$]; for timing [$F (1, 32) = 9.25$, $p < .005$]; and for duration [$F (1, 32) = 4.73$, $p < .05$]. No curvilinear expectation effects were evidenced. Table 5.5 presents the means associated with each dependent variable for each expectation level.

Control over content and timing showed situation effects for content [$F (4, 64) = 13.69$, $p < .0001$]; and for timing [$F (4, 46) = 14.28$, $p < .001$]. Underlying each of these effects was a strong initiator distinction: more control over content and timing was reported for teacher than student initiations: for content [$F (1, 64) = 50.93$, $p < .0001$]; and for timing [$F (1, 64) = 43.84$, $p < .001$]. The initiator distinction proved nonsignificant for the duration-control question, although means were in a direc-

TABLE 5.6   Study III Teachers' Interaction Control Perceptions for Each Classroom Situation

	Type of Control		
Classroom Situation	*Subject Matter*	*Timing*	*Duration*
Public with hands raised	5.15	4.67	4.90
Public with no hand	5.10	5.21	4.83
Child initiation in public	4.56	4.28	4.80
Teacher initiation in private	5.18	5.35	4.91
Child initiation in private	4.46	4.18	4.73

tion similar to the other control questions. The setting (public/private) distinction was nonsignificant for all three types of control. Table 5.6 presents the means associated with these analyses.

Discussion

Perceptions of control were found to be related to teacher-performance expectations for the student and to who initiated the interaction. Interactions with high-expectation students were seen as more controllable than those with low-expectation students. Also, teacher initiations were seen as more controllable than student initiations. Finally, and as before, the interaction setting (public vs. private) appeared to have the weakest relation to control perceptions. These results support the Expectation Communication Model and replicate the studies reported earlier.

The effects of type of interaction and the student involved on control have now been tested on three distinct samples: a heterogeneous group of teachers with varying types of teaching experience (from primary school learning disability classrooms to high school); a homogeneous group of fourth-grade departmentalized teachers; and a sample of third- through sixth-grade teachers in the same school district who were also aware that their interactions with rated students had been observed. The consistency of results indicates that the relations between perceptions of control, performance expectations, and interaction initiator are of broad generality.

STUDY IV.   INTERACTION CONTROL AND CLASSROOM BEHAVIOR

So far, most of the relations suggested by the Expectation Communication Model have received empirical support. Perhaps the most important relations, however, have not yet been investigated. What remains to be shown is that interaction control perceptions relate to teacher feedback in the predicted manner. Providing such a test was the primary objective of this fourth and final study. To test control-feedback relations, hypothesis 3 was stated as three specific predictions. Because the between- and within-class distinction is scrutinized in this study, each prediction is first stated as a between-class phenomenon and then as a within-class phenomenon:

1. A teacher's perception of interaction control will be negatively related to the teacher's use of criticism; or the students over whom teachers feel least control will also be the students most often criticized.
2. A teacher's perception of interaction control will be positively correlated with the teacher's use of praise; or the students over

whom teachers feel most control will be the students most often praised.

3. A teacher's perception of interaction control over students will be negatively correlated with the teacher's ignoring student responses; or the students over whom teachers feel least control will also be the students whose responses are most often ignored by the teacher.

In prediction 3, teacher ignoring student responses was viewed as a mildly aversive event for the student and was therefore predicted to show a relation similar to criticism. It was necessary to use ignoring as a proxy for negative affect because the incidence of verbal criticism in classrooms was typically quite low (see Chapter 4).

As was the case in earlier studies, hypotheses were tested through correlation, not manipulation. Also, for exploratory purposes, control perceptions were related to the frequency of other types of classroom interaction in addition to feedback.

Method

Observed Behaviors. For each of the twelve students, the per-hour frequencies of eleven interactions with the teacher were related to teacher-control perceptions. These included six situations:

1. Teacher-initiated public interaction
2. Student-initiated public interaction
3. Teacher-initiated private interaction
4. Student-initiated private interaction
5. Teacher-initiated procedural interaction
6. Behavioral intervention

In addition, each student had a per-hour frequency of two categories of appropriateness:

1. Correct or appropriate
2. Incorrect or inappropriate

Finally, each student had a per-hour frequency for the following three types of feedback:

1. Relative praise
2. Relative no feedback
3. Relative criticism

A detailed definition of each behavior is provided in Chapter 2.

Within-Classroom Relations Involving Control Perceptions and Behavior. For within-classroom relations, teacher responses to the PCQ were summed for each student separately. Since three types of control were assessed in five situations, each student's total PCQ score was based on responses to fifteen questions. Total scores could then range from zero to ninety, with ninety representing the greatest possible perceived control. The average student PCQ score was 72.31 (SD = 5.05), indicating (1) that the average teacher response was slightly less control than "a large amount" and (2) that there was comparatively little variation in teacher-control beliefs. One teacher answered all PCQ questions with the same response ("A large amount of control"), necessitating her removal from the within-classroom analysis. A measure of the internal consistency for the individual student PCQ measures demonstrated acceptable reliability (Cronbach's Alpha = .77).

The eleven interaction measures for each student were constructed using the procedures outlined in Chapter 2.

Between-Classroom Relations Involving Control Perceptions and Behavior. A measure of *general dyadic interaction control* felt by the teacher was created by averaging the total PCQ scores for the twelve target students. It should be kept in mind that this measure described the teacher's general perception of control over twelve students in the class, not over the class as a whole group. Since the measured classroom behaviors were dyadic in nature, this restricted definition seemed appropriate.

The average behavior frequency for the twelve observed students served as the measure for the *classroom-behavior frequency.* In the case of negative feedback (criticism and no evaluation), extremely low average frequencies were observed (.05 and .03, respectively). The associated standard deviations were of an almost equal magnitude (.06 and .03, respectively). This indicated that in some classrooms little or no negative feedback occurred during the observation periods. This restriction in range suggests that correlations involving these variables essentially test for differences between classrooms in which negative feedback did and did not occur.

Analytic Design. The correlation approach outlined in Chapter 3 was employed. For within-class control-behavior relations, individual student scores were paired and correlated separately for each class. The average correlation indicated the average within-class relation for the sample. For inference testing, the correlations were converted to Z scores and *t*-tested against a hypothetical value of zero.

For between-classrooms analyses the average control and behavior scores for each classroom were paired and correlations were calculated to gauge covariation in pairs. This procedure describes the bivariate association with regard to general differences in entire classrooms. Significant correlations indicate that a greater-than-zero relation exists when general classroom differences are at issue.

Results

Control-Affective Feedback Relations. Table 5.7 presents the results of all control-behavior relations and tests. First, control-feedback relations within classrooms revealed that no feedback frequency was significantly associated with perceptions of control over individual students within the classes. One trend was evidenced, however. Students over whom the teacher felt greater control were least likely to have initiations go unevaluated [$\bar{r} = -.13$, $t(15) = 1.78$, $p < .10$]. No between-classroom relation reached or approached significance.

Control-Interaction Frequency Relations. Table 5.7 also reveals that none of the four within-class relations involving control and the frequency of academic settings proved significant. There was, however, some tendency for students over whom teachers felt greater control to ask relatively fewer questions in private [$\bar{r} = -.14$, $t(15) = 1.70$, $p < .12$]. In addition, whereas the average correlation did not depart significantly from zero,

TABLE 5.7 Relations between Teachers' Perceived Control of Interactions and the Frequency of Observed Classroom Interactions

Teacher Perception of Interaction Control and Frequency of:	Within Classrooms		Between Classrooms	
	Average Correlation	p	Correlation	p
Praise following an appropriate response	+.02	...	−.10	...
Criticism following an inappropriate response	+.04	...	+.37	.19
No evaluation following any response	−.13	.10	+.37	.19
Teacher initiations in public	+.07	...	−.25	...
Teacher initiations in private	−.08	...	−.50	.04
Student initiations in public	.00	...	+.28	...
Student initiations in private	−.14	.12	+.36	.16
Teacher procedural initiations	−.08	...	−.32	...
Teacher behavior interventions	−.18	.05	+.03	...
Appropriate responses	+.12	.09	−.26	...
Inappropriate responses	−.15	.09	−.14	...
Total responses	−.05	...	−.24	...

eleven of the sixteen classrooms revealed negative relations between control and teacher-initiated private interactions. In general, then, there was some indication that high control over a student may be associated with less private interaction.

Also, within classrooms, behavioral interventions were significantly negatively associated with perceived control $[\bar{r} = -.18, t (15) = 2.13, p < .05]$, and eleven of sixteen classrooms also showed a negative relation between procedural interactions and control. Therefore, greater control over a student tended to be associated with relatively less nonacademic contact. In addition, more control over a student tended to be associated with more appropriate responding $[r = .12, t (15) = 1.84, p < .09]$ and less inappropriate responding $[\bar{r} = -.15, t (15) = 1.85, p < .09]$.

Between classrooms, the frequency of only one academic setting was found to significantly covary with control: the less control a teacher reported over students, the more frequently the teacher initiated academic interactions in private $[\bar{r} = -.50, df = .16, p < .04]$. Whereas this was the only significant result, the general pattern in correlations did seem to indicate that teachers who felt greater control tended to have more student initiations and fewer teacher initiations in their classrooms.

Discussion

Relations of Control to Affective Feedback. To be consistent with the Expectation Communication Model, the within-classroom relation between control and praise was predicted to be positive and the relations between control and criticism and no evaluation were predicted to be negative. Study IV found that all feedback-control relations were uniformly small and only one relation even approached significance. Within classrooms there was some tentative evidence indicating that lesser control over a student covaried with more frequent ignoring of a student response.

At least four explanations can be offered for the weakness in control-feedback relations. First, several sampling restrictions in the study tended to limit the variability in control perceptions. Normal classrooms in primarily middle-class schools participated, and this sample included only volunteering teachers and consenting students. It is likely that each sampling restriction tended to remove lower-control students from consideration. This speculation is borne out by the generally high control perceptions reported over all students in the study. In the general discussion of the study's results (Chapter 9), this restriction in sampling will again be discussed.

Second, the general frequency of affective feedback, especially negative affect, was quite low. This presents another sampling restriction in that the estimates of the affect each student received were insensitive. Future research might (1) lengthen the amount of classroom observation time, (2) have classroom coders attempt to infer the degree of positive or negative affect present in every teacher-student interaction (rather than only code obvious affective expressions), and/or (3) measure students' perceptions of teacher affect (see Chapter 7).

Third, it is important to realize that while the PCQ measures control perceptions with no attention paid to subject matter, science and social studies lessons were the primary subjects observed. Had mathematics and reading lessons also been coded (where one could reasonably expect the sharpest degree of differential teacher behavior), stronger relations might have appeared. This possibility is further discussed in Chapter 9.

Finally, it must be recognized that only one teacher cognition was measured in this study. Teacher affective reactions to students are linked to a variety of goals other than optimizing interaction control (cf. Good, 1980). Efforts to relate clusters of teacher beliefs to classroom behavior may reveal more complex relations than a single measure.

Relations of Control to Frequency of Interactions. The control–frequency-of-interaction relations was also quite weak, perhaps for some of the same reasons offered above.

Within classrooms, more teacher control over a student was associated with fewer behavioral interventions and tended to be associated with more appropriate responding, less inappropriate responding, and less student initiation in private. Between classrooms, more teacher general dyadic control was associated with less teacher private academic initiation.

Summary and Conclusions

While all the significant relations and trends were consistent with the Expectation Communication Model, the general lack or weakness of relations was troubling. This suggested that modification in the personal control links of the model may be necessary. A discussion of such modification will be delayed until the final chapter, however, so that these revisions can take advantage of insights generated in the chapters that follow.

6

Teacher Attributions for
Student Performance

Chapter Overview

Chapter 6 contains four studies involving teacher attributions for student performance. In Study I a new system for coding open-ended teacher attributions is described, which divided causal explanations into twelve categories. Study II then examined some causal dimensions underlying these categories and their effect on behavioral intentions. Study II indicated that teachers distinguished causes not only by internality and stability but also by the degree of teacher involvement implied by them. For instance, teachers reported feeling more of a personal role in successes when "interest in the subject matter" was the cause for performance than when "physiological processes" (i.e., mood, health) was the cause. In Study III, some earlier attribution findings were retested with the new system. Most notably, the low-expectancy cycle was reconfirmed: teachers tended to discount the successes of low-expectation students by attributing them to external causes. Finally, in Study IV, the system was used to relate causal attributions to classroom praise and criticism within the primary sample of classrooms. Surprisingly, it was found that students who received the most praise from teachers were those whose successes were most often attributed by teachers to their own behavior (i.e., directions and instruction, the task). This relation was found to be stronger for low- than high-expectation students.

Objectives of Attribution Research

One objective for the study of attribution is identifying the causal categories and underlying dimensions used to explain behavior. As Heider (1958) argued, what is needed is "the construction of a language that will allow us to represent, if not all, at least a great number of interpersonal relations, discriminated by conventional language in such a way that their place in a general system will become clear" (p. 9).

A second objective for attribution study is the determination of how causal ascriptions influence subsequent behaviors (Weiner, 1977a). If research in related areas (most notably, attitudes) is to provide an example, we should expect that the attribution-behavior link will be both subtle and complex (cf. Brannon, 1976). Such complexity implies that our ability to accomplish the second objective is dependent on achieving the first. That is, the sensitivity and accuracy of our cognitive measurements will determine the upper limit of relations involving that measurement, regardless of the importance of underlying constructs (Nunnally, 1978). It seems, then, that the dual purposes of accurately describing peoples' causal analyses and of generating powerful attribution models which explain the nuances of affect and behavior are mutually dependent tasks.

Goals of the Present Studies

The present chapter reports four studies relevant to expectation communication and attribution theory. The first study had three goals: (1) to review coding systems for free-response academic attributions; (2) to supplement this literature by presenting a new categorization scheme based on the responses of professional teachers; and (3) to suggest a synthesis of the new and previous schemes.

The second study had a set of goals which relate to the potential uses of the new scheme for uncovering the attribution-behavior link. These goals were (1) to suggest three dimensions which capture the attribution distinctions most relevant to teacher-student interactions; (2) to test teachers' awareness of a newly proposed dimension; and (3) to relate the new dimension to behavioral intentions.

With the new scheme in hand, a third study attempted to replicate earlier attribution findings involving teacher expectations.

The fourth and final study employed the coding scheme in an attempt to relate teacher expectations and attributions to teacher use of feedback. The first three studies were originally reported by Cooper and Burger (1980); the fourth study has not been previously reported. Study IV is also the only one to involve the sample of teachers described in Chapter 2.

STUDY I.   CONSTRUCTING A MEASURE OF CAUSAL ATTRIBUTIONS

The original conceptualization concerning academic attributions and their underlying dimensions was provided by Weiner and his associates (Weiner, Frieze, Kukla, Reed, Rest, and Rosenbaum, 1971). Following Heider

(1958), these authors suggested that four attribution categories (ability, task difficulty, effort, and luck) were "the most common and general of the perceived causes of success and failure" (Weiner, 1977b). Two dimensions were said to underlie these categories: internal (ability, effort) vs. external (task, luck) and stable (ability, task) vs. unstable (effort, luck). The internality dimension was proposed as controlling personal affective responses and interpersonal evaluations. The stability dimension was seen as controlling both personal and interpersonal expectancy shifts. Empirical evidence supporting this conceptualization has frequently been reported (see Weiner, 1977a; Bar-Tal, 1978).

Whereas this analysis provided a substantial beginning, Weiner (1974) stated that he and his associates recognized "a number of deficiencies in the classification scheme" (p. 6). Specifically, it was felt that a stable-effort category (i.e., the cause was a general disposition toward laziness or industry) and a category which allowed for ability improvements were missing. Considering these deficiencies, Frieze (1976) presented an inductively based coding scheme for open-ended responses. The causal explanations used were generated by fifty-one college students who were asked to explain success and failure at academic and non-academic tasks for both self and others. This scheme contained eight attribution categories: ability, effort, task, luck, other person, mood, stable effort, and unclassifiable.

Bar-Tal and Darom (1979) also categorized free-response attributions. In this case, responses were provided by sixty-three fifth-grade students and attributions referred to performance on an actual examination. These authors described eight categories, arrived at with the restriction that each contained at least 5 percent of the total attributions. These eight categories were: ability in the subject matter, efforts exerted during the test, interest in the subject matter, difficulty of the test, difficulty of the material, preparation for the test at home, teacher explanation of the material, and conditions in the home.

Interesting similarities and dissimilarities exist between the two coding schemes. However, a gap exists in the populations used to generate them. Specifically, a professional teaching population has not been asked for free-response attributions concerning the performance of their own students. This gap might restrict the generalizability of any system based on the two studies alone and might limit their applicability to the study of teacher-expectation communication.

A synthesis of three systems might provide a categorization scheme which, if reliable, could be used for open-ended responses by most academic populations. Methods could then be standardized for research across a wide variety of problems and populations. In addition, forced-choice alternatives could be generated that would provide participants with an adequate richness of alternatives.

Method

Participants. Participants were obtained from graduate education courses at the University of Missouri, Columbia. Thirty-nine of the forty-three teachers asked to participate agreed to do so. All participants had taught elementary or secondary school for at least 1 year with a mean of 5.9 years of experience. Eighteen teachers reported teaching at the primary school level (K to 6), fourteen reported teaching at the secondary level (7 to 12), and seven reported teaching special-education classes.

Procedure. Each teacher received a booklet containing written instructions and the questionnaire items. Instructions were:

> Students vary in many ways. However, on the following pages we are concerned only with academic performance. Academic performance can be defined as the quality of performance in terms of tests and class exercises with academic content. In your class(es) you undoubtedly had students who were consistently either high or low in academic performances.

Teachers were asked to list the initials of three students from their most recent class(es) whom they expected to do well academically and three whom they expected to do poorly. The teachers were then given four pages, each referring to a success or failure by one student group, and each page had eight numbered lines on which to list why the outcomes occurred. The order of presentation of the four situations was randomized across participants. At the bottom of each page teachers were told:

> Now that you have listed the reason(s), go back to the percentage column and indicate what percentage of the (high/low) expectancy students' (successes/failures) were caused by each explanation. Remember that the total of your percentage estimates should not exceed 100 percent.

Finally, participants filled out a page of items asking for their teaching background and experience.

Scoring. In a manner similar to Orvis, Kelley, and Butler (1976), the responses from the first twenty-three teachers were examined by coders for similarities and dissimilarities. The coders did not know which experimental situation was associated with each response. The coders were also unaware of the earlier categorization schemes. The seventeen categories shown in Table 6.1 emerged from this examination.

Some responses include words and phrases applicable to more than one category. The rule used was that responses would be placed in the category described first unless the following words or phrases clarified its meaning.

The responses of the remaining sixteen teachers were then scored by one of the original coders and by another scorer who was unfamiliar with

TABLE 6.1   Keyword Coding for Attribution Categories

Academic ability (11 percent): Ability, intelligence, reading, creativity, comprehension, skill

Previous experience (6 percent): Previous/past experience, success at a task before, subject knowledge, previous practice/success, readiness, repeated practice/success, success in related areas

Habits (3 percent): Study habits, listening habits/skills

Attitudes (6 percent): Attitudes, feelings/liking of/toward school/subject.

Self-perception (2 percent): Maturity, relates well to others

Physical or emotional ability (3 percent): Physical ability, emotional stability, hyperactivity

Typical effort (20 percent): Interest, motivation, concern, gives up, effort, willingness, good listening, enthusiasm, participation, applying self/knowledge, desire, eager, laziness, wants to succeed, bored, did not try, worked on own, competition

Immediate effort (8 percent): Carelessness, completeness of assignment, being prepared, did each assignment, took time to have questions answered, overcame distractions, rushed without thinking, hurried

Attention (8 percent): Attention, concentration, preoccupation, day-dreaming, out of touch with reality, concern with other things, distractability

Directions (3 percent): Did/could follow directions, understood directions, understood what was expected

Mood (3 percent): Mood, having a good day

Task (7 percent): Task, work, material, steps too large, new/different material/task, amount, no reading involved, long time period

Instruction (7 percent): Individual attention, teacher, adequate explanation, good directions, extra help, good instruction

Family (3 percent): Parents, family, home, background, outside school support.

Other students (3 percent): Outside interference, helped by others, group interaction, student/peer assistance

Miscellaneous external (1 percent): Health, repetition, use of other materials, class too large, wrong grade, luck, other

---

Note. Examples of positive instances only are presented. Approximate percentages of total citations for each category appear in parentheses. About 5 percent of the total attributions were unclassifiable.

the research objective. Both coders used the criteria (key words) provided in Table 6.1. These scorers agreed on 73 percent of the responses, a figure that compares favorably with earlier studies (cf. Frieze, 1976; Orvis et al., 1976). When disagreements occurred, a third coder was used to determine category placement.

Results and Discussion

The seventeen categories generated from teacher responses are presented in Table 6.2, column C. Columns A and B contain the categories offered by Frieze (1976) and Bar-Tal and Darom (1979). The suggested synthesis of schemes appears in column D.

   Obviously, the three schemes share an academic ability category. The present study, however, also retained distinctions between other internal,

TABLE 6.2   A Summary of Previous Coding Systems and a Suggested Synthesis

A *Frieze(1976)*	B *Bar-Tal and Darom* *(1979)*	C *Seventeen Categories*	D *A Synthesis*
Ability	Ability	Academic ability	Ability (academic,
Stable effort	Effort during Test	Physical and	physical, or
Immediate effort	Preparation at	emotional ability	emotional)
Task	Home	Previous experience	Previous experience
Other person	Interest in the	Habits	Acquired
Mood	subject matter	Attitudes	characteristics
Luck	Difficulty of test	Self-perceptions	(habits, attitudes,
Other	Difficulty of	Maturity	self-perceptions)
	material	Typical effort	Typical effort
	Conditions in the	Effort in	Interest in the subject
	home	preparation	matter
	Teacher explanation	Attention	Immediate effort
	of the material	Directions	Attention
		Instruction	Teacher (quality and
		Task	kind of instruction,
		Mood	directions)
		Family	Task
		Other students	Other students
		Miscellaneous	Family
			Physiological processes
			(mood, health)

stable characteristics (i.e., physical or emotional ability, previous experience, self-perceptions, habits, and attitudes). It is suggested that in a synthesis of schemes three categories replace these six. A general "ability" category would include academic, physical, and emotional abilities, with academic ability its most significant component. The "previous-experience" category would be retained since a substantial percentage of attributions fell into this category. A third category, called acquired characteristics, would include habits, attitudes, and self-perceptions. This suggestion takes into consideration both parsimony and the need for a category which implies that ability improvements are possible (Weiner, 1974).

With regard to effort attributions, Frieze (1976) found stable-effort and immediate-effort categories while Bar-Tal and Darom (1979) described three effort-related categories: interest in the subject matter, effort on the test, and preparation at home. For the synthesis "typical-effort," "immediate-effort," and "interest-in-the-subject-matter" categories have been retained. The "interest" category was generated for the present data from the typical-effort category by making the key words "interest," "enthusiasm," and "good listening" a separate unit. The interest distinction has two nice features: (1) it divides the largest of the original categories in half and (2) it presents an intriguing developmental possibility. That is, in younger students, interest in the subject matter may be viewed as an internal but unstable factor, whereas in older students, it may be viewed as internal and stable. This shift in meaning would be different from the typical-effort category, whose use might increase with age but whose dimensionality would always be the same (internal stable).

Bar-Tal and Darom's (1979) differentiation of "preparation at home" and "effort on the test" was not retained because the category (1) did not appear in this study or the Frieze (1976) study and (2) had no immediately apparent theoretical significance, as in the case of interest. Finally, the effort-related category of attention was retained from the present study because of its large percentage of teacher citations.

Regarding external unstable causes, Bar-Tal and Darom's elementary school students produced a distinction between the "difficulty of material" and the "difficulty of tests." This distinction was not retained here for the same reasons as those cited for "home effort." It is interesting to note, however, that fifth-grade students produced the "finest" causal distinctions between elements most immediate to the testing situation itself. This suggests that the events of greatest importance to people may be perceived as having the most causal elements. Other researchers might opt, in working with young students, to retain these distinctions and collapse the immediate-effort and attention categories, which did not differentiate with youngsters.

Other people figured in all three schemes. For the synthesis, three distinctions were retained: the teacher (a collapsing of "quality and kind of instruction" and "directions"), other students, and family. These distinctions seemed intuitively important, considering the differing roles each group plays in the academic process. A twelfth and final category, physiological processes, was also retained. This encompassed the mood and maturity categories and health attributions from the miscellaneous external category.

External unstable causes posed a problem. There was no evidence that the typical indicator of this category, "luck," was used with any frequency as an explanation for academic outcomes. Bar-Tal and Darom (1979) did not present a luck category, Frieze (1976) reported luck attributions only in nonacademic settings, and luck was cited only 0.4 percent of the time in this study. Further, no attribution exhibiting the clear external unstable characteristics of luck appeared to replace it. "Other students" came closest, but this category has features of both an ephemeral and continuing nature. These findings suggest that in academic situations, attributions do not exhibit a complete crossing of internality and stability. Rather, internality is a dimension which runs from extremely internal (ability) through a person/environment mixture (interest in the subject matter) to extremely external (the task). Stability, on the other hand, is restricted in range, running from extremely stable (ability) to a stable unstable mix (other students).

Having redefined the seventeen categories into twelve, it was necessary to reassess the reliability of coding free responses. To accomplish this, two naïve coders were asked to place each key word into a category using only the labels presented in Table 6.2, column D, as definitions. This is an exceptionally conservative reliability test in that the labels represent the minimum amount of information a coder would have available. The key words themselves represented 83 percent of the total free-response attributions. This procedure led to absolute agreement rates of 63 and 69 percent. When the agreements were weighted with regard to how many free-response attributions the key word represented, the agreement percentages rose to 81 and 86 percent. Finally, Cohen's Kappa (Cohen, 1960) was computed for each coder, using the original classification as criteria. These coefficients of intercoder reliability equaled .60 and .66.

STUDY II.   UNCOVERING THE DIMENSIONS UNDERLYING ATTRIBUTIONS

With the twelve free-response attribution categories in hand, the discernment of a smaller number of dimensions along which the causes differed was next attempted. Most important in this search was the potential relevance of discriminations for future teacher behavior.

In addition to internality and stability, at least two other dimensions have been offered as underlying attributions. First, Rosenbaum (Note 6.1) proposed that intentionality, or whether the act was seen as purposive, distinguished causal attributions. Abramson, Seligman, and Teasdale (1978) suggested that the global vs. specific referent of causes was relevant to the development of learned helplessness. As an alternative to these, we chose to investigate the varying implications attributions seemed to contain about the role the teacher played in the performance. Such a dimension might shed further light on the personal control notions addressed in the previous chapter. That is, the twelve categories connoted differing degrees of teacher participation or involvement in the outcome. As the most striking example, it seemed that perceiving the cause of performance was "the student's family" connoted much less of a teacher role than, for example, the causes of "task" or "attention." This seemed to hold both across the internality and stability dimensions and between attributions *within* any two-dimensional combination.

Study II was undertaken, then, to determine (1) whether the teacher involvement implied by each of the twelve attributions was recognizable by teachers, and (2) whether this dimension helped explain variation in three kinds of behavioral intentions.

TABLE 6.3   Predicted Relations between Attributions and the Teacher-Involvement Dimension

	High Teacher Involvement	*Low Teacher Involvement*
Internal Stable	Acquired characteristics Typical effort Interest in the subject matter[1]	Ability Previous experience
Internal Unstable	Interest in the subject matter Immediate effort attention	Physiological processes
External	Task Teacher	Other students Family

[1]Interest in the subject matter can be viewed as either stable or unstable.

Table 6.3 presents the hypothesized differences in teacher role connotations of attributions within the internality and stability dimensions. For example, it was predicted that for internal unstable attributions, teachers would feel the least influence over a performance if the cause was "physiological processes." Teachers can generate interest, attention, and effort through actions prior to a student's performance. Altering physiological processes is much less likely.

In addition to testing for awareness of the teacher-involvement dimension, Study II also examined three teacher-classroom-behavior intentions. Prospective teachers were asked (1) how a particular causal explanation would influence their intended feedback to the student (i.e., praise and criticism), (2) whether the outcome and attribution would lead to a change in their style of teaching, and (3) whether they would work with the student more or less based on the supposed cause of performance.

Method

Participants.   Sixty-two predominantly female education students served as volunteers. All participants were enrolled in a class required for teacher certification. Therefore, it was assumed that participants either had teaching experience or were planning to become teachers.

Independent Variables.   Each participant was asked to complete a questionnaire. Participants were randomly assigned to two conditions: half read about a successful student and half read about a student described as having performed poorly. Questionnaire instructions were as follows:

> Assume you are a teacher of a fifth-grade class. You have just given an examination and you find that one of your students had performed extremely

(well/poorly). On the next pages, twelve possible reasons for this (success/failure) are given. You are asked to tell how you would respond to the student in light of the (success/failure) and the cause for it.

The participants were then presented in a random order with the twelve causal explanations uncovered in Study I.

Dependent Variables. After each explanation, the participants were presented with the following four questions:

1. How much of a role did you play in the (success/failure)?
2. How strongly would you (praise/criticize) the student?
3. Would you work more or less with the student?
4. Would you change the way you taught the student or the kinds of tests you gave the student?

   Participants were asked to respond to each question on an 11-point scale. Higher numbers indicated a large role (for question 1) or a more active behavior intention (for questions 2, 3, and 4).

Results

Awareness of the Teacher-Involvement Dimension. To determine whether the twelve attribution categories were distinguished by teachers in terms of their implied teacher involvement, a two-way mixed-model analysis of variance was conducted on responses to the question: "How much of a

TABLE 6.4   Individual Attribution Means for Teacher-Involvement Measure

| | *Outcome* | | |
Attribution	*Success*	*Failure*	*Mean*
Ability	5.43	4.84	5.13
Previous experience	4.03	5.75	4.88
Acquired characteristics	5.83	4.59	5.21
Typical effort	5.70	5.28	5.49
Physiological processes	4.50	2.94	3.72
Interest in the subject	6.63	6.59	6.61
Attention	6.83	4.47	5.65
Immediate effort	6.73	1.94	4.33
Task	5.23	7.50	6.36
Teacher	8.67	9.12	8.89
Other students	5.33	4.66	4.99
Family	3.87	2.37	3.12
Mean	5.73	5.00	5.37

role did you play in the (outcome)?". Performance outcome (success/failure) served as the between-subjects variable and attributions (twelve categories) served as the within-subjects variable. The means associated with this analysis are presented in Table 6.4.

Participants reported playing a larger role in success than in failure [F (1, 60) = 4.81, $p < .04$]; and also registered different magnitudes of perceived involvement dependent on the suggested cause of performance [F (11, 660) = 30.09, $p < .04$]. An outcome-by-attribution interaction [F (11, 660) = 11.42, $p < .0001$] indicated that for some causes perceived teacher involvement was more dependent on performance outcome than for other causes.

Since attributions varied with regard to involvement implications, it was necessary to consider whether this dimension was distinct from internality and stability. Specific comparisons could have been used to test the hypothesized relations concerning within-cell differences portrayed in Table 6.3. Instead, Tukey Honestly Significant Difference critical values (Myers, 1972) were generated and used to test all pairwise comparisons of attributions within the internality by stability cells. Because the outcome-by-attribution interaction was significant, the critical values were generated for twenty-four mean comparisons. Comparisons were then carried out within outcome conditions.

In the success condition, as Table 6.5 shows, no differences were found between the teacher-involvement implications of internal stable attributions. However, the internal unstable causes of attention, immediate effort and interest in the subject matter, were seen by teachers as implying more of a personal role than physiological processes (all p's $< .01$). The three high teacher-involvement causes did not differ from one another. Finally, the external cause of teacher was seen as implying more of a personal role than the external causes of other students, task, and family (all p's $< .01$). The latter three causes did not differ.

As with success, the failure condition revealed no differences between teacher-involvement implications of internal stable causes. For internal unstable causes, interest in the subject matter implied a greater teacher role than attention, physiological processes, and immediate effort (all p's $< .01$). Externally, the categories teacher and task surpassed both family and other students in perceived teacher influence ($ps < .01$). Finally, the reported teacher role was smaller when the family was the cause than when other students ($p < .01$) were cited.

Three attribution categories (attention, immediate effort, and task) showed noticeable changes in their teacher involvement implications dependent on performance outcome. To explore this shift, each attribution was compared with itself across outcome conditions. The success/failure main effect was removed (by subtracting .73 from the success mean) before comparisons were performed, but a statistically significant difference for immediate effort ($p < .01$) and task ($p < .01$) remained.

TABLE 6.5   Obtained Relations between Attributions and the Teacher-Involvement Measure

| | Outcome | | | |
| | Success | | Failure | |
Attribution Dimension	High teacher involvement	Low teacher involvement	High teacher involvement	Low teacher involvement
Internal stable	Acquired characteristics Typical effort Ability Previous experience		Typical effort Ability Previous experience Acquired characteristics	
Internal unstable	Interest in the subject Immediate effort Attention	Physiological processes	Interest in the subject	Attention[1] Physiological processes Immediate effort
External	Teacher	Other Students Task Family	Task Teacher	Other students Family[2]

Note.   Attributions at differing ends of the teacher involvement dimension were predicted to differ or were found to do so ($p < .01$).
[1] Attention implied more involvement than immediate effort ($p < .01$).
[2] Family implied less involvement than other students ($p < .01$).

TABLE 6.6 The Relations between the Five Attribution Categories and Classroom-Behavior Intentions

Attribution	Success Outcome			Failure Outcome		
	Praise	Change Teaching	Work More	Criticism	Change Teaching	Work More
Internal/stable	7.69a	3.95a	5.61	3.08b	6.72b	8.18a
Internal/unstable/teacher involved	8.18a	3.43ab	6.06	3.12b	6.87b	7.18b
Internal/unstable/teacher uninvolved	6.97b	3.70a	5.73	4.78a	5.43c	6.83b
External/teacher involved	7.67a	2.76b	5.96	1.66c	8.23a	8.26a
External/teacher uninvolved	6.54b	4.20a	5.85	1.99c	5.39c	7.44b
F value (df = 4,116)	8.99	4.61	1.13	35.11	19.30	10.80
p level	.0001	.002	ns	.0001	.0001	.0001

Note. Higher scores mean intention to do more of the behavior. Differing subscripts within each dependent variable denote significant mean differences by the Newman-Keuls test.

In sum, five attribution distinctions seemed to emerge: internal/
stable; internal/unstable/teacher involved; internal/unstable/teacher uninvolved; external/teacher involved; and external/teacher uninvolved.

Relations between Attribution Dimensions and Behavior Intentions. In
order to analyze the behavior intention questions, the twelve attributions
were collapsed into the five distinctions mentioned above and displayed in
Table 6.6. The three intention questions were first subjected to one-way
multivariate analyses of variance with separate analyses conducted for
success and failure conditions. Each analysis contained a single within-
teacher independent variable (five attribution cells) and three dependent
variables. The MANOVAs produced significant attribution effects for
both success, $\lambda = .655$ [$F (12, 301) = 4.37, p < .001$] and failure, $\lambda = .271$
[$F (12, 323) = 17.20, p < .0001$]. Six univariate ANOVAs (one for each
measure and each outcome condition) followed. Table 6.6 presents the
means, associated F-test values, p-levels, and the results of Newman-
Keuls comparisons.

With regard to feedback following failure, there was a greater intention to use criticism expressed in the internal/unstable/teacher involved
condition than in any other condition ($p < .01$). Failure caused by external events (whether or not the teacher was involved) led to the least intention to criticize (p's $< .01$). For success, participants intended greater
positive feedback in both teacher-involved cells than in the corresponding
teacher-uninvolved cells (p's $< .01$).

With regard to the second intention measure, participants reported
the largest intent to *change* the way they taught in the external/teacher-
involved cell, when the outcome was a failure ($p < .01$). For success,
there was least intention to change ($p < .05$) when the cause was the
teacher.

Teacher intent to *work more* with the student proved influenced by
causes only in the failure condition. For failure, internal stable and exter-
nal/teacher-involved causes led to a greater intention to work with the
student than did other attributions (p's $< .01$).

Discussion

The Teacher Involvement Dimension. The results of Study II indicated
that differing attributions have differing teacher-involvement implications. Essentially five attribution categories emerged such that the external and internal/unstable categories needed to be further broken down
into teacher-involved and -uninvolved causes. Also, the attributions immediate effort and task revealed different teacher-involvement implications for success and failure outcomes. Immediate effort implied more
teacher involvement in success than failure. This may have occurred be-

cause an immediate effort cause for success implies teachers have been effective motivators and a failure implies they have been ineffective. Task implies more teacher involvement in failure than success. Perhaps, when teachers perceive the task as causing failure, they assume a deliberate attempt was made to challenge the student with difficult material.

The Behavioral Intentions.   Turning next to the behavior intentions, intended use of praise can most parsimoniously be described as determined by perceived teacher involvement. If the cause of success implied little teacher influence, less intention to positively reinforce the student was expressed. For criticism, involvement and internality proved crucial. Internal/unstable/teacher-involved causes elicited the greatest intention to criticize. In this condition, the teachers' self-image as a motivator may be most severely threatened.

The intention to change teaching style was also predominantly a matter of perceived teacher involvement. If a successful performance was caused by something implying a relatively large teacher role, little change in teaching style was intended. For failure, a large teacher role led to the most intended change.

Finally, internal/stable causes for failure led teachers to express the strongest intention to spend more time with the student. Surprisingly, external/teacher-involved causes led to an equally strong intention. Thus if the teacher saw a failure as potentially avoidable through personal intervention, both altered and more intensive behavior intentions resulted.

STUDY III.   EXPECTATIONS AND ATTRIBUTIONS

As part of the initial data collection, teachers were asked to supply four causal profiles. Interpretations of the successes and failure of both high- and low-expectation students were obtained from each teacher. After supplying attributions, teachers assigned percentages indicating the proportion of cases to which the cause was applicable. This technique allowed some experimental questions to be asked of the attribution data.

Specifically, the data were examined for what Weiner (1977a) called the "low expectancy cycle." This is the tendency for teachers to discount the successes of low-expectation students by attributing them to external or internal unstable causes. Such a discounting of success can have detrimental effects on students. For instance, if a low-expectation student's performance shows marked improvement but the teacher fails to consider changes in abilities, stable effort, or habits and attitudes as potential causes for the improvement, then the external or unstable attribution can become a mechanism for sustaining expectation effects (see Chapter 1). The student may perceive that he/she is not given personal credit for success and this may work to mitigate the student's motivation to succeed. In this manner teacher attributions can serve to prevent positive improvements in performance.

Cooper and Lowe (1977) have demonstrated the low-expectancy cycle. They asked professional teachers to rate the influence three kinds of students had over their own performance. These researchers reported that high-expectation students were seen as more personally responsible for success than lows. While lows were seen as more responsible for failure, the difference proved statistically unreliable. The authors speculated that underlying these failure differences may be a teacher perception that high-expectation students fail because of lack of effort (unstable) while lows fail because of lack of ability (stable). The present data provide an opportunity to retest the original findings and to test the authors' interpretation.

Method

Data-Analysis Strategy.   Teachers in Study I gave each student a percentage score for each of the twelve attribution categories. If a category was not cited by the teacher, a percentage of zero was recorded. If the causal category was cited, the percentage given by the teacher was used. In this manner, 48 percent scores were generated for each teacher, one for each of twelve attributions in each of four conditions (high- or low-expectation student for success or failure).

In addition to these within-teacher variables, a between-teacher classification was also employed. After completing the questionnaire, participants were asked to state the grade level at which they taught and how many years teaching experience they had. From these responses, five teacher types were generated: elementary school/inexperienced (1 to 4 years, $n = 9$); elementary school/experienced (over 4 years, $n = 9$); secondary school/inexperienced ($n = 5$); secondary school/experienced ($n = 9$); and special education ($n = 7$). Thus, the final design represented a $5 \times 2 \times 2$ complete crossing, with twelve dependent variables (attributions).

Results

First, the results of a multivariate analysis of variance revealed a statistically significant expectation main effect [$\lambda = 0.391$; $F (12, 23) = 2.98, p < .02$]; outcome main effect [$\lambda = 0.392$; $F (12, 23) = 2.97, p < .02$], and expectation-by-outcome interaction [$\lambda = -.175$; $F (12, 23) = 9.01, p < .0001$]. All multivariate effects associated with the teacher background variables proved nonsignificant and were not followed by univariate ANOVAs.

The twelve attribution categories were then separately examined

TABLE 6.7   Percent Attribution Citations for Each Teacher Expectation by
Performance-Outcome Condition

	Ability Main Effects	
Cause	*High-Expectation Means*	*Low-Expectation Means*
Effort in Preparation	9.67	4.76
Task	3.78	9.35
Typical Effort	11.40	15.44

	Outcome Main Effects	
Cause	*Successful-Outcome Means*	*Failure-Outcome Means*
Previous Experience	9.04	4.74
Effort in Preparation	2.37	12.06
Attention	3.72	11.91

	Outcome × Ability Interactions[1]			
	High-Expectation Success	*Low-Expectation Success*	*High-Expectation Failure*	*Low-Expectation Failure*
Ability	21.41a	3.03b	3.97b	22.82a
Acquired Characteristics	14.69a	3.20b	6.03ab	9.62ab
Typical Effort	12.33ab	7.05b	10.46ab	23.82a
Interest in the Subject	6.28ab	14.84a	8.84ab	5.56b
Effort in Preparation	1.79b	2.91b	17.53a	6.59b
Task	1.79b	16.00a	5.77b	2.69b
Teacher	5.64b	19.00a	15.51a	3.26b

[1] Differing subscripts for interaction effects denote significant mean differences by the New-man-Keul test.

through two-way analyses of variance. The means associated with this analysis are presented in Table 6.7.

Expectation Main Effects.   Three statistically significant expectation main effects were found. Teachers attributed the cause of the performance to "effort in preparation" more often for high- than low-expectation students [$F(1, 34) = 4.47, p < .05$]. On the other hand, the task [$F(1, 34) = 7.97, p < .01$] and typical effort [$F(1, 34) = 6.40, p < .02$] were seen as responsible for low-expectation students' performance more often than for high-expectation students' performance.

Outcome Main Effects.   Three significant outcome main effects were found. Teachers attributed successful performances more often than unsuccessful performances to previous experience [F (1, 34) = 4.00, $p <$ .05]. On the other hand, teachers attributed student failures more often than student successes to effort in preparation [F (1, 34) = 21.33, $p <$ .0001] and attention [F (1, 34) = 10.38, $p < .003$].

Interactions.   Seven significant expectation-by-outcome interactions were revealed: ability [F (1, 34) = 32.28, $p < .0001$]; interest in the subject matter [F (1, 34) = 6.96, $p < .02$]; effort in preparation [F (1, 34) = 6.63, $p < .02$]; task [F (1, 34) = 12.19, $p < .005$]; teacher [F (1, 34) = 15.10, $p < .0005$]; and typical effort [F (1, 34) = 6.15, $p < .02$]. Newman-Keuls tests were conducted for each of these interaction effects.

Teachers saw the cause of performance as student ability more often for high-expectation student success and low-expectation student failure than in the other two conditions ($p < .01$). The opposite pattern was found for the teacher attribution. Teachers attributed the cause of performance to themselves significantly more often in the low-expectation student success and high-expectation student failure conditions than in the other two conditions ($p < .05$). Teachers also saw the cause of high-expectation student success as acquired characteristics more often than they did for low-expectation student success ($p < .05$). Low-expectation student success was more often attributed to interest than was low-expectation student failure ($p < .05$). Teachers attributed high-expectation student failure to effort in preparation significantly more often than for any other condition ($p < .01$). Teachers also believed that the task was responsible for low-expectation student success more often than for students in the other three conditions ($p < .01$). Finally, teachers attributed low-expectation student performance to stable effort more often when the student failed than when the student succeeded ($p < .05$).

Discussion

Before evaluating the results with regard to the goals of the study, an unexpected finding deserves mention. No significant effects were found for the other students, family, or physiological processes causes. All other attribution categories were affected by at least one source of variance. Two possible explanations for this finding can be offered. First, the results may be a statistical phenomenon. The three uninfluenced causes were the lowest in percentage use, meaning variation in responses would be difficult to uncover. Second, and more interestingly, this result may imply that each of these causes is in some way *luck*-related. That is, getting ill, one's mood, and one's classmates or family may be seen, at least in part, as being *produced* by chance. Put more specifically, each cause might be considered beyond the control of all parties involved. This interpretation might explain the missing external unstable cell. While luck attributions may rarely be made in academic contexts, the chance *origin* of other internal unstable and external stable causes may play an important role in the way others are perceived. Such a state of affairs would dictate the exhibited even distribution of these citations across conditions.

In terms of the stated hypotheses, the present data replicated the Cooper and Lowe (1977) findings and illustrated the low-expectancy cycle. Most dramatically, low-expectation student successes were attributed to either internal unstable or external causes over 52 percent of the time. While these attributions may be veridical at any moment, if a teacher does not periodically explore other causes for lows' successes, a sustaining expectation effect may result.

The data also supported Cooper and Lowe's (1977) speculation about what attributions underlied the personal-responsibility differences. High-expectation student failure was more often attributed to immediate effort while low-expectation student failure was perceived more often as ability-caused.

STUDY IV.   ATTRIBUTION-FEEDBACK RELATIONS

Study IV was the most pivotal undertaking for testing the validity of the Expectation Communication Model. The previously reviewed findings, involving teacher expectations, perceptions of control, and attributions, have primarily examined how different sets of cognitions might fit together in the teacher's cognitive world. Presently, in the link between a teacher's perceived causes for student performance and their use of affective feedback, the teacher communicates to the student the content of this cognitive nexus. In doing so, the teacher's perceptions of the student becomes a factor in the student's self-perceptions and attitudes toward future achievement. This communication is the crucial link in interpersonal expectation phenomena and marks a transition from a focus on teacher processes to a focus on student processes. Thus, Study IV, tests the relation between teacher attributions for student performances and actual classroom use of praise and criticism.

The prediction made by the Expectation Communication Model presented in Chapter 1 is straightforward: high-expectation students' affective feedback from teachers will be more contingent on teacher perceptions of student effort on the task (with effort meaning an internal unstable cause) than will low-expectation students' feedback. This may be the case because the relative lack of control over interactions teachers feel with lows dictates that feedback be used more often to control the context of the next interaction.

Implicit in the prediction is the notion that interaction control is the primary concern of teachers in classrooms. In this vein, Cooper and Baron (1979) wrote:

It is also suggested the effort is *not* the dominant contingency for ongoing classroom evaluation. Personal responsibility, in general, and effort in particular, are meaningful only when an overriding concern with classroom management has been satisfactorily resolved. More specifically, only when the teacher has determined that feedback will not alter a perceived state of high personal control will the student responsibility implication of an act become the dominant influence on feedback. [p. 276]

For our purposes, this statement actually contains two hypotheses. One hypothesis addresses a within-class relation and one an interaction of the between- and within-class levels of analysis. First, and most importantly, it is predicted that students over whom teachers feel greater interaction control will receive more effort-contingent feedback than their low-control classmates. This is strictly a within-class relation and the central unifying link in the expectation communication process.

Second, Cooper and Baron (1979) imply that unless the teacher senses some minimal amount of control over interactions with a student, attributions to student effort may rarely, if ever, appear as a reinforcement contingency, regardless of the student's relative control or expectation standing in the class. To clarify with an example, it is likely that classrooms exist in which even students who perform relatively better than their classmates give their teacher an unsatisfactory sense of control. Certain special-education classrooms may generate in teachers uniformly low sets of expectations, meaning that control is almost always an issue in interactions. In these classrooms, we would suggest most reinforcement is a function of behavior-management considerations, even if the performance to which the feedback refers is strictly academic in nature. Here a kind of basement effect exists: relatively high expectations within the class will still be quite low in an absolute sense. To take the opposite and more appealing case, there should also exist classrooms which generate in teachers a satisfactory sense of control over all students. In these instances, the amount of effort-contingent feedback would be high and potentially indistinguishable for both high- and low-control students within the class. If such minimal- and optimal-control classrooms exist, then our initial hypothesis needs modification. That is, Cooper and Baron's second suggestion implies that relative differences in teacher expectations within a class will mediate feedback contingencies only so long as the general classroom expectation is neither very high or very low. In such cases, control considerations either apply to none or apply equally to all.

In the present study, the optimal-control circumstance is probably the one most closely describing the present sample of classrooms. As Chapter 5 presented, teachers in participating classrooms expressed a high degree of perceived control over students. Indeed, a problem with the control measurements was that they generated little variability in teacher responses. We expected, therefore, to uncover fairly high effort-feedback relations in our sample of classes. However, general control over all students was less than optimal, so it may be possible to uncover a within-class difference in effort-feedback relations for high- and low-expectation students.

Six specific predictions were made for Study IV:

1. Within classrooms, the amount of praise a student received from a teacher would be positively related to the percentage of that student's successes the teacher felt were caused by immediate effort.
2. Within classrooms, the amount of criticism a student received would be positively related to the percentage of that student's failures the teacher felt were caused by a lack of immediate effort.
3. Within classrooms, the relations in number 1 would hold more strongly for high- than for low-expectation students.
4. Within classrooms, the relation in number 2 above would hold more strongly for high- than for low-expectation students.
5. Between classrooms, the general amount of praising a teacher engaged in would be positively related to the average percentage of effort attributions the teacher made for her students' successes.
6. Between classrooms, the general amount of criticism a teacher employed would be positively related to the average percentage of failures the teacher felt were caused by a lack of immediate effort.

While these hypotheses guided our analyses, we also examined the relations between other attributions and classroom feedback patterns.

Method

Participants and Procedures. The participants in this study were the teachers described in Chapter 2. In the fashion described in Study I, teachers provided open-ended attributions. Teachers then assigned percentages to each cause dependent on how frequently the attribution explained the student's performance. Attributions were collected concurrently with the three classroom observation periods.

The teacher attribution questionnaire responses were categorized by two scorers who were blind concerning all other data in the study. Interrater reliabilities for placing attributions into the twelve categories as indicated by Cohen's Kappa coefficients were .89, .77, and .86 for the three administration periods. When the original coders disagreed on the coding of an item, a third rater was used to determine classification.

TABLE 6.8   Categories Used to Relate Teacher Attributions and Affective Feedback

A. Attribution Categories
   1. *Internal stable causes*
      Ability
      Previous experience
      Acquired characteristics
      (habits, attitudes,
      self-perception)
   2. *Stable effort causes*
      Stable effort
      Interest in the subject matter

   3. *Immediate effort causes*
      Immediate effort
      Attention
   4. *Teacher-related causes*
      Directions and instructions
      Task
   5. *Other external causes*
      Family
      Other students

B. Affective-feedback categories[1]

Teachers' relative use of affect following a student response

	High		Low	
	High Teacher Expectation	*Low Teacher Expectation*	*High Teacher Expectation*	*Low Teacher Expectation*
High				
Low				

[1] Teachers and students were categorized separately for praise and criticism and for each time of the school year.

Attribution Measures.   Causes were placed into one of the eleven categories, as shown in Table 6.8.A (The physiological processes category did not appear in the study). The eleven attributions were further reduced to five more substantive types. Each of the twelve students in each class thus had ten percentage scores. The percentages referred to the frequency with which the teacher felt the student's successes and failures were caused by (1) internal stable, (2) stable effort, (3) immediate effort, (4) teacher-related external, or (5) miscellaneous external causes. These five categories roughly match the five categories suggested in Study II. The exception is that the internal-unstable categories were replaced by stable-effort and immediate-effort categories. This was done for purposes of creating measures with appropriate variability for statistical analysis.

Feedback Measures (see Table 6.8.B).   To investigate the relations between success attributions and praise, classrooms were first grouped according to whether the teacher used a large or small amount of *praise per appropriate response*. That is, teachers were not classified according to absolute frequency of praise. Instead, teacher average praise usage was first residualized with the average appropriate responses in the classroom used as predictor. Residuals were then used to assign teachers to either a high- or low-praising group. A similar procedure was used to classify students within each classroom into high- and low-praise receivers. That is, within each classroom separately, the praise residual from appropriate responses were used to categorize students. For failure-attribution analyses, criticism and ignoring of responses provided a composite residualized measure to place teachers and students into groups. Frequency of criticism was residualized on inappropriate responses and no evaluation was residualized on total responses. The residuals were then summed and a median split performed, both between and within classrooms. The residualization procedure means comparisons are between the relative likelihood, *on any single response*, of giving or receiving affect.

Expectation Groups. Two within-class expectation groups were formed. The six students who teachers ranked highest on verbal ability and general potential formed the high-expectation group and the six ranked lowest formed the low-expectation group.

Analytic Design. The categorization procedure described above was undertaken to prepare the data for repeated-measures analysis of variance. Since two of the variables were predicted to interact, it was felt that the ANOVA procedure would be simplest to interpret and present (see Chapter 3).

In essence, students were categorized as to (1) whether their teacher generally used more or less praise or criticism than other teachers, (2) whether they received generally more or less praise or criticism than their classmates, and (3) whether their teacher had relative high or low expectations for them. This meant one between- and two within-class distinctions would be tested.

Since the classroom was used as the unit of analysis, two other assumptions about the data seemed appropriate. First, the two within-class variables were treated as repeated measurements of a single unit. This meant that classrooms (or teachers) were assumed to have been researched under four stimulus-student conditions (high- vs. low-praise receiver crossed by high- vs. low-performance expectation). High vs. low general teacher use of praise was assumed to be a between-units variable. While the hypotheses predicted that the two within-classroom variables would statistically interact, the analytic design also allows a test of statistical interaction between levels of analysis. However, while Cooper and Baron suggested a cross-level three-way interaction (i.e., the effort-feedback relation difference for high- and low-expectation students would appear only in moderate-control classrooms), no such interaction was predicted here. This was because all the classrooms sampled appeared to exhibit homogeneously moderate to high teacher perceptions of control.

Approximately three students fell into each cell of the design, but this was not always the case. To correct for this, the average attribution for the students in each cell was used as a single data point to represent the classroom (or teacher). This is similar to performing an unweighted ANOVA to correct for unequal cell sizes.

Rather than add time of the school year (fall/winter/spring) to the design as yet a third repeated measure, the analyses of the attribution data were conducted separately for the three observation periods. This was done so that classrooms and students could be reclassified at each time of the year.

Results

Between-Classroom Relations. The analyses of attributions for successful outcomes revealed no noteworthy between-class relations. Causal citations and teacher general frequency of praise dispensation were essentially unrelated. None of the five causal categories produced results meeting or approaching significance criteria.

The between-classroom effects for failure attributions and criticism proved to be much more interesting. Table 6.9 presents the means underlying two apparent relations between teachers' general criticism usage and their causal perceptions. First, teachers who used the most criticism tended to feel student failures were less often caused by deficiencies in internal stable factors (fall $[F (1, 14) = 2.75, p < .13]$; winter $[F (1, 13) = 4.10, p < .07]$; spring $[F (1, 14) = 3.43, p < .09]$). Although this trend never reached significance, the fact that the analysis was quite conservative (see Chapter 3) and that the trend appeared at all three times of the school year indicated it deserved further attention. Second, in winter, teachers who used the most criticism were those who most often felt their

TABLE 6.9 Between-Classroom Relations Involving a Teacher's Average Use of Negative Feedback and Average Citation of Different Causes for Failure

Percentage of Student Failures Attributed to:		Teacher's Use of Negative Feedback	
		Less Than Other Teachers	*More Than Other Teachers*
Internal-stable causes (lack of	Fall	20.3	9.8
ability; inexperience; bad habits	Winter	29.4	13.9
and attitudes)	Spring	34.0	14.9
Immediate-effort causes (lack of	Fall	37.3	47.6
attention; not being prepared for	Winter	34.7	60.0
the task)	Spring	38.0	35.3

TABLE 6.10 Relations Involving a Teacher's Average Use of Praise, the Teacher's Relative Expectation for Students, and the Teacher's Citation of Different Causes for Success

| | Teacher's Average Use of Praise | | | |
| | More Than Other Teachers | | Less Than Other Teachers | |
Percentage of Students' Successes Attributed to	High-Expectation Students	Low-Expectation Students	High-Expectation Students	Low-Expectation Students
Stable-effort causes (stable effort; interest in the subject matter)				
Fall	6.30	1.17	5.55	7.02
Winter	8.43	1.85	12.62	14.82
Spring	14.98	8.16	0.38	3.46

student failures were caused by a lack of immediate effort [F (1, 13) = 4.70, $p < .05$]. In spring, these means were roughly equal and in fall, they were again supportive of an a priori prediction, but not significantly so. In general, then, both the internal-stable and immediate-effort results are consistent with the Weiner et al. (1971) attribution model.

Table 6.10 presents the means associated with an uncovered statistical interaction between teacher general praise usage and their performance expectations for students in their class. The attribution involved is the stable-effort factor (i.e., general industry and interest in the subject matter). It was found that teachers who used the most praise felt their high-expectation students' successes were more often caused by stable effort than were their low-expectation students' successes. On the other hand, low-praise-using teachers felt lows' successes were caused by stable effort more so than were highs' successes. This interaction was significant in winter [F (1, 13) = 6.89, $p < .03$] and approached significance in fall [F (1, 14) = 4.03, $p < .07$].

Within-Classroom Relations.   Several relations involving attributions for success and whether a student received more or less praise than his or her classmates deserve mention. First, the relation between immediate effort and praise displayed in Table 6.11 was *opposite* to the prediction. At all times of the school year, students who received the most praise were least likely to have immediate effort cited as the cause of success. This relation only approached significance in spring, however [F (1, 14) = 3.01, $p < .11$]. Also unpredicted was a high- vs. low-praise–receiver main effect for the external teacher-related category and an interaction between praise-receiving and performance expectations for this same category. The underlying means are presented in Table 6.12.

First, and in general, students whose successes were seen by their teachers as more often caused by high teacher-involvement factors were also students who received the most praise. This relation appeared as a trend in fall [F (1, 14) = 3.20, $p < .10$] and was significant in winter [F (1, 13) = 9.68, $p < .01$] with consistent means in spring. The significant in-

TABLE 6.11   Within-Classroom Relations Involving a Teacher's Relative Use of Praise toward Different Students and the Teacher's Citation of Different Causes for the Student's Success

		Student's Reception of Praise	
Percentage of Student's Successes Attributed to:		*Less Than Other Students*	*More Than Other Students*
Immediate effort (paying	Fall	26.7	24.2
attention; being prepared for the	Winter	33.6	32.5
task)	Spring	28.3	22.8

TABLE 6.12 Within-Classroom Relations Involving a Teacher's Relative Use of Praise toward Different Students, the Teacher's Relative Expectation for Students, and the Teacher's Citation of Different Causes for Student Success

| | Teacher's Expectation for the Student | | | |
| | Higher Than Other Students | | Lower Than Other Students | |
Percentage of Students' Successes Attributed to	More Praise Than Other Students	Less Praise Than Other Students	More Praise Than Other Students	Less Praise Than Other Students
Teacher-related causes (followed directions; good instruction; appropriate tasks)				
Fall	5.23	4.06	21.94	15.21
Winter	2.92	0.67	30.01	11.71
Spring	11.40	11.25	25.08	20.04

teraction revealed that the strength of this within-class relation may be mediated by the teacher expectation for the student. At all three times of the school year, low-expectation students showed the relation between teacher involvement and praise to a greater degree than did high-expectation students. The interaction reached significance only in winter, however [F (1, 13) = 11.29, $p < .005$]. If praise in classrooms is dependent on high teacher involvement, this may be more the case for low-than for high-expectation students.

Three success attribution categories produced significant level-of-expectation main effects. These means are presented in Table 6.13. At all three times of the school year, internal stable factors were seen as more often causing high-expectation student successes: for fall [F (1, 14) = 5.78, $p < .04$]; for winter [F (1, 13) = 21.60, $p < .005$]; for spring [F (1, 14) = 5.57, $p < .04$]. Teacher-related factors and other external factors were more often seen as causing low-expectation student successes: for teacher-related, in fall [F (1, 14) = 9.18, $p < .01$]; winter [F (1, 13) = 9.31, $p < .01$]; spring [F (1, 14) = 3.58, $p < .09$]; for other external, in fall [F (1, 14) = 3.03, $p < .11$]; spring [F (1, 14) = 5.70, $p < .04$]; with consistent means in winter. These results are consistent with those found in Study III and again demonstrate the low-expectancy cycle.

Finally, the analyses of failure attributions revealed only one within-classroom effect, in addition to the interaction mentioned earlier. At all three times of the school year deficiencies in internal stable factors were seen as more often the cause of low- than high-expectation student failures: for fall [high M = 10.77 vs. low M = 19.35; F (1, 14) = 9.46, $p < .01$]; for winter [high M = 17.78 vs. low M = 26.11; F (1, 13) = 24.59, $p < .001$]; for spring [high M = 21.16 vs. low M = 25.73, n.s.]. This result is also consistent with Study III.

TABLE 6.13 Within-Classroom Relations Involving a Teacher's Relative Expectation for Students and the Teacher's Citation of Different Causes for Student's Success

		Teacher's Expectation for the Student	
		Higher Than Other Students	*Lower Than Other Students*
Internal stable causes (ability;	Fall	44.97	30.29
previous experience; acquired	Winter	44.59	21.71
characteristics)	Spring	39.26	23.61
Teacher-related causes (followed	Fall	4.65	18.57
directions; good instructions;	Winter	1.79	20.86
appropriate tasks)	Spring	11.32	22.56
Other external causes (family;	Fall	2.00	4.49
other students)	Winter	1.41	3.89
	Spring	1.98	3.46

Discussion

The results of Study IV produced quite a few unexpected findings, which should not be too surprising, since the study represents an attempt to relate attributions and feedback in a considerably more naturalistic setting than has been the case in previous work.

With regard to variation among classrooms, trends were found which indicated that teachers who used more criticism per interaction were those who less often cited internal-stable causes and more often cited immediate-effort causes for student failure. These were the only results that were predicted and are consistent with achievement attribution theory (cf. Weiner et al., 1971).

The results pertaining to within-classroom processes were quite different. There was some indication that students who were most freely praised were those whose successes were least often due to immediate-effort causes. A somewhat stronger finding was that students who were praised most often were those whose successes were seen as owing to teacher-related causes. The more frequently a student's successes were seen as implying a positive teacher influence the more freely the student was praised, relative to other classmates. In addition, the strength of this relation was mediated by the teacher expectation for the student performance. The degree to which praise and teacher-related causes covaried was greater for low- than for high-expectation students.

In general, the results supported the notion that feedback may be contingent on student effort when the teacher's general classroom reinforcement strategy is at issue. This seems reasonable, since these averages may not be responsive to the daily requirements of classroom management. Rather, the teacher may set the general level of affect in a class based on a positive value for greater effort and use reinforcement intentionally to encourage strong effort. When one examines how teachers distribute reinforcement within a class, however, there is no evidence that these deviations from the mean are effort-related. Rather, students whose causes for success most often implied the teacher had a positive influence were given freest praise.

From this data, then, what conclusions can be drawn about attribution theory and expectation communication? First, this study demonstrates the strong explanatory value of Weiner and colleagues' (1971) achievement attribution theorizing. The data also generally support the Expectation Communication Model. In a manner perhaps even stronger than suggested by the model, the teacher's concern for personal influence emerges from the data. The model proposed that the reinforcements received by high-expectation students might be more contingent on effort than the reinforcements received by lows. This relation did not appear but another potentially supportive relation did emerge. It was found that low-expectation student feedback may be more contingent than highs' feedback on following teacher directions and working at appropriate tasks. Lows appeared to be learning that their successes are caused more often than highs' successes by help from and obedience to the teacher. Clearly, these cognitions would lead to the distinction in highs' and lows' sense of personal control proposed by the model.

Perhaps the finding that greater within-class praise was associated with a teacher belief that they personally influenced more of the student's successes should not have been surprising. Indeed, in Study II of this chapter, it was found that prospective teachers expressed a behavioral intention to positively reinforce successes that they believed they personally caused. This congruence in intention and behavior (though different people were involved) should lend added credibility to the result.

Also encouraging is the reemergence of the notion of teacher control as a potential influence on reinforcement. The reader will recall that disappointingly small relations were found (in Chapter 5) between teacher-perceived interaction control and feedback. In this study, it was found that a teacher's perception of involvement in how the student is doing does in fact play a role in rewards. A detailed discussion of why the Personal Control Questionnaire did not uncover control-feedback relations and the attribution measure did will be postponed until our general discussion of all findings in Chapter 9.

Finally, it is important for the reader to be aware of a methodological assumption which is implicit in the Study IV analyses. Our examination of reinforcement contingencies proceeded as though we were discussing a *within-student* phenomenon. That is, we assumed that based on these data, if a low-expectation student's success is caused by teacher-related factors, the performance is more likely to be praised than another success by the same student caused by other factors. But the study did not measure attributions after particular performances. Rather, we asked questions about student performance in general and related this to an aggregate feedback measure. The distinction is much like that between the two classroom levels of analyses, except that here we are examining between- and within-*student* phenomena. Some caution in this inferential leap is appropriate. The problem is an extremely difficult one, however, because obtaining within-student data in naturalistic settings seems nearly impossible. Asking a teacher for attributions after each classroom performance would be an unreasonable interruption and would undoubtedly affect the process under study (cf. Dweck and Gilliard, 1975). A possible recourse would be to use a stimulated recall methodology (Marland, Note 6.2). In any case, interpretations of the present results should keep this limitation of our data in mind.

7

Teacher and Student Perceptions of Interaction Frequencies

Chapter Overview

This chapter examines a class of variables that the Expectation Communication Model did not include: teacher and student awareness of the frequency of classroom interactions. If teachers lack awareness of the frequency with which events occur, they may unintentionally differ in their behavior toward high- and low-expectation students. Similarly, if students perceive teacher behavior as related to expectations, it may affect motivation and achievement regardless of the perception's accuracy.

In Study I, teacher expectations and student gender were related to teacher and student perceptions of the frequency of classroom interactions. Perceptions of high- and low-expectation students were found to parallel the differences in interaction frequencies suggested by the model as underlying the expectation communication process. Teacher perceptions were also found to be congruent with model predictions, except for praise: Teachers reported praising lows more frequently than highs.

In Study II, student and teacher perceptions of the frequency of classroom events were compared with one another and with those of classroom observers. It was found that teachers in this study agreed with observers in their perceptions of classroom-behavior frequencies. Students also agreed with observers but not nearly as closely as did teachers.

Perceptions of Interaction Frequency

The Expectation Communication Model contained the proposal that observable differences in teacher behavior were related to differences in the self-concept and academic performance of students. The model contained no mention, however, of whether teachers and students are aware of behavior frequency differences and what role such awareness may play in classroom relations. This chapter is an attempt to address these issues.

STUDY I. EXPECTATIONS AND PERCEPTIONS OF INTERACTION FREQUENCIES

Knowing whether or not teachers are aware of differences in their behavior toward different students may shed light on the motivations behind expectation effects. Specifically, it was suggested in Chapters 1 and 5 that different behavior toward high- as opposed to low-expectation students was probably a "spontaneous" reaction and teachers were most likely unaware of such systematic behavior differences. Although it was argued that teachers may attempt to enhance personal control by inhibiting the public initiations of lows, it was *not* assumed that such behavior was a conscious strategy.

Finding that teachers were poor describers of their differential behavior toward highs and lows would be consistent with this "unmotivated" interpretation of teacher-expectation effects. Alternatively, a finding that teachers were good describers of their own behavior would support a conclusion that (1) the differences were intentional or (2) the differences were unintentional but possibly not within the teacher's control.

Student awareness of differences in teacher behavior toward highs and lows could play a direct role in expectation communication. If teachers behave differently toward students but students are unaware of the discrimination, the impact of the actual difference may be mitigated. Likewise, students who believe they are treated differently may respond to this perception regardless of its veridicality.

Weinstein and Middlestadt (1979) performed the only previous investigation into student perceptions of how teachers treat high and low achievers. These researchers found that students perceived teachers as treating highs more positively, as demanding more from highs academically, and as providing highs with more frequent chances to perform. On the other hand, lows were perceived as receiving greater teacher concern and vigilance. These student perceptions are quite congruent with model predictions.

In Study I, teacher and student perceptions of how frequently different types of classroom interactions occur were measured and these were related to teacher expectations and student gender. The present study differs from Weinstein and Middlestadt's (1979) in that they had students describe the treatment of hypothetical high and low achievers, whereas in this study students described their own treatment. It was hypothesized that the perceptions of interaction frequency differences would parallel the observed interaction differences described in Chapter 1 (from previous research) and/or Chapter 4 (from the present research).

Methods

Expectations and Gender. The procedures for obtaining teacher-expectation and student-gender information can be found in Chapter 2.

Student Perceptions. In the spring, students filled out a questionnaire which assessed their beliefs about how frequently they were involved in classroom interactions. The questionnaire was designed to sample students' perceptions of interactions that observers were coding in the project.

Students were asked to respond to the following questions (the corresponding observed behaviors are noted in parentheses):

1. How often does your teacher call on you to answer a question? (Teacher initiated public interaction.)
2. How often does the teacher come to your desk to look at your seatwork? (Teacher initiated private interaction.)
3. How often do you raise your hand to tell your teacher and the class something when the teacher has not asked a question? (Student initiated public interaction.)
4. How often do you go to the teacher to ask her a question about your seatwork? (Student initiated private interaction.)
5. How often do you give the correct answer when your teacher calls on you during class? (Appropriate response.)
6. How often does your teacher give you praise for something you do in class or tell you that you did well? (Absolute praise.)
7. How often does your teacher ignore what you say in class? (Absolute no evaluation.)
8. How often does your teacher criticize your answer when you say something in class? (Absolute criticism.)
9. How often does your teacher speak to you about misbehaving in class, such as when you're talking or not doing your work? (Behavorial intervention.)

For each question, students had three response options: more often than classmates (scored 3); about the same amount as classmates (scored 2); and less often (scored 1) than classmates. Several questions were repeated at different points in the questionnaire. For purposes of data analysis, these responses were combined. Other questions were asked only once because of time limitations and possible response ambiguity. In all cases, higher scores were associated with the belief that the student personally took part in more such interactions with the teacher than with other students.

Teacher Perceptions.   Teachers were asked to fill out a parallel questionnaire for each of the twelve target students in their classrooms. The corresponding questions presented to the teachers were:

1. How often do you call on this student to answer a question? (Teacher initiated public interaction.)
2. How often do you go to this student's desk to look at his/her work? (Teacher initiated private interaction.)
3. How often does this student raise a hand to tell you and the class something when you have not asked a question? (Student initiated public interaction.)
4. How often does this student come to you to ask a question about seatwork? (Student initiated private interaction.)
5. How often does this student respond with the correct answer when you call upon him/her? (Appropriate response.)
6. How often do you give this student praise for something he/she does in class or tell the student he/she did well? (Absolute praise.)
7. How often do you ignore (not comment upon) the student's answer to a classroom question? (Absolute no evaluation.)
8. How often do you criticize the answers of this student when he/she says something in class? (Absolute criticism.)
9. How often do you have to speak to this student about his/her misbehavior? (Behavioral intervention.)

Teachers had the same three options as students to choose from in responding to each question. For example, in response to question 8, teachers could choose: (1) I criticize this student more often than I criticize other students (scored 3); (2) I criticize this student about the same amount as I criticize other students (scored 2); and (3) I criticize this student less often than I criticize most other students (scored 1). Teachers were asked each question only once.

Data-Analysis Strategy.   The ANOVA approach described in Chapter 3 was employed. Teacher-expectation level (high/average/low) and student gender served as "independent" variables and the eighteen teacher and student perceptions served as dependent variables. Because teachers and students were asked to assess interaction frequencies *relative to classmates*, only within-classroom relations could be addressed.

Results

Expectations. Table 7.1 presents the means and F values for expectation effects on teacher perceptions of interaction frequencies. Several interaction frequency perceptions were found related to expectations. Specifically, as expectations for a student's performance increased, teachers also reported (1) more frequent teacher initiation in public [F (1, 30) = 80.20, $p < .001$], (2) less frequent teacher initiation in private [F (1, 30) = 41.67, $p < 001$], (3) more frequent student initiation in public [F (1, 30) = 42.00, $p < .001$], (4) more frequent appropriate responding [F (1, 30) = 101.25, $p < .001$], and (5) less frequent teacher use of criticism [F (1, 30) = 9.87, $p < .005$]. In addition, two teacher perceptions of differences in interaction frequency approached significance. Higher expectations tended to be associated with (1) less frequent student initiation in private [F (1, 30) = 3.70, $p < .08$] and (2) less frequent absolute praise [F (1, 30) = 3.14, $p < .09$]. Two other teacher perceptions of behavior (teacher ignoring of responses and behavior interventions) were not related to performance expectations.

TABLE 7.1 Teacher Perceptions of Interaction Frequencies for Each Level of Teacher Expectations for Students

	High	Average	Low	F test	p level
Teacher initiations in public	2.31	1.98	1.47	80.20	.001
Teacher initiations in private	1.58	1.94	2.33	41.67	.001
Student initiations in public	2.22	1.84	1.53	42.00	.001
Student initiations in private	1.56	1.75	1.81	3.70	.08
Appropriate responding	2.62	2.08	1.50	101.25	.001
Absolute praise	2.03	2.02	2.24	3.14	.09
Absolute no evaluation	1.88	1.78	1.77	< 1	ns
Absolute criticism	1.70	1.94	2.14	9.87	.005
Behavioral interventions	1.71	1.85	1.71	< 1	ns

Note. F-test values are based on 1 and 30 degrees of freedom. All F-tests pertain to linear expectation effects.

Student perceptions of interaction frequencies revealed four significant expectation differences, presented in Table 7.2. Students for whom teachers expressed higher expectations saw themselves as engaging in (1) more frequent teacher-initiated public interactions [F (1, 30) = 20.4, $p < .001$], (2) less frequent teacher-initiated private interaction [F (1, 30) = 8.85, $p < .01$], (3) more appropriate responding [F (1, 30) = 21.20, $p < .001$] and (4) less frequent criticism from the teacher [F (1, 30) = 5.31, $p < .03$]. One trend was uncovered: higher teacher expectations tended to be associated with a student perception of more praise from the teacher [F (1, 30) = 3.71, $p < .07$].

TABLE 7.2   Student Perceptions of Interaction Frequencies for Each Level of Teacher Expectations

	High	*Average*	*Low*	*F test*[1]	*p level*
Teacher initiations in public	3.80	3.58	3.11	20.4	.001
Teacher initiations in private	2.97	3.12	3.48	8.85	.01
Student initiations in public	1.61	1.52	1.48	1.00	ns
Student initiations in private	1.66	1.74	1.84	2.15	ns
Appropriate responding	4.50	4.02	3.83	21.20	.001
Absolute praise	3.99	3.72	3.68	3.71	.07
Absolute no evaluation	1.58	1.64	1.70	1.34	ns
Absolute criticism	2.94	3.19	3.47	5.31	.03
Behavioral interventions	3.33	3.20	3.50	1.00	ns

[1] *F*-test values are based on 1 and 30 degrees of freedom. All *F* tests pertain to linear expectation effects.

Gender.   A total of four significant gender effects appeared. Table 7.3 presents the means underlying these effects. Teachers viewed boys as making fewer appropriate responses than girls [$F(1, 15) = 4.52, p < .05$] and receiving more criticism than girls [$F(1, 15) = 22.45, p < .001$]. Boys thought they received less praise [$F(1, 15) = 8.60, p < .01$] and more behavioral interventions [$F(1, 15) = 6.12, p < .03$]. There was also a tendency for teachers to think that boys initiated fewer private interactions than did girls [$F(1, 15) = 3.79, p < .07$].

TABLE 7.3   Gender Differences in Perceived Interaction Frequencies

Interaction Frequency Perceptions	*Males*	*Females*
Student perception of absolute praise	3.56	4.02
Student perception of behavioral interventions	3.64	3.05
Teacher perception of student-initiated private interactions	1.59	1.82
Teacher perception of student appropriate responding	1.96	2.18
Teacher perception of criticism	2.21	1.65

Note. All effects are significant.

Finally, two expectation levels by gender interactions emerged. The relevant data are presented in Table 7.4. Two expectation main effects reported above, that teachers perceived highs as receiving fewer teacher-initiated private interactions and less praise, was, apparently, was more true for boys than for girls [for interactions $F(2, 30) = 3.36, p < .05$; for praise $F(2, 30) = 6.31, p < .005$].

Discussion

Teacher perceptions of the frequency of interactions were generally consistent with the Expectation Communication Model's predictions and with

TABLE 7.4 Expectation Level by Gender Interactions in Perceived Interaction Frequencies

	Males			Females		
	High	*Average*	*Low*	*High*	*Average*	*Low*
Teacher perceptions of teacher-initiated private interactions	1.50	2.00	2.49	1.66	1.88	2.22
Teacher perception of praise	1.88	2.09	2.28	2.19	1.94	2.19

the observed patterns of behavior reported in Chapter 4. There was one notable exception, however. The model predicted and observations found that high expectations for students were associated with more frequent praise from the teacher. Teachers, however, tended to report praising low-expectation students more than highs. This finding can be interpreted in two ways. First, it could be argued that teachers' report were influenced by self-presentation concerns: teachers might think that reporting that they use less praise with lows would indicate bias against less-able students. This self-presentation explanation is contradicted, however, by (1) the general accuracy of teacher reports about other behaviors and (2) the teachers' willingness to report using more criticism with lows. The second interpretation is that teachers' perceptions of praise toward highs and lows are unintentionally inaccurate. Part of this inaccuracy may be due to the previously offered notion that most reactions to student work are spontaneous. This explanation accounts for inaccuracy but it does not explain the teachers' "erroneous" belief that lows receive *more* praise. Perhaps, this belief stems from greater teacher awareness when praise to lows occurs. Praise to highs may be more routine and therefore more easily forgotten.

Student perceptions of interaction differences showed a *perfect* congruence with the model's predictions. All relational directions were as specified and more than half reached or approached significance. Thus, a pattern of behaviors consistent with the notion that teachers use feedback to channel interactions with low-expectation students into controllable contexts (i.e., teacher-initiated or private exchanges) was perceived by students. Indeed, the student perceptions contain stronger support for the model than the observational data presented in Chapter 4. Why this is so is not entirely clear. It is possible that students exaggerate interaction differences or that the observational data was less sensitive to actual differences than student perceptions. Whatever the cause, it appears expectation effects are perceived by students as very real phenomena.

Perception differences between the sexes were minimal and this result is consistent with the findings of Weinstein and Middlestadt (1979). As previously noted (Chapter 4), this may have been partly due to the fact that boys and girls were selected from within teacher expectation groups and different expectations may explain much of the gender effect.

However, the two expectation level by gender interactions indicated some expectation effects were stronger for boys than for girls. This substantiated Brophy and Good's (1974) notion that boys were generally more salient in classrooms than were girls.

STUDY II.   THE CONGRUENCE OF INTERACTION PERCEPTIONS

Study I examined perceived differences in the treatment of high- and low-expectation students. Study II examined the related issue of the general "match" of teacher and student interaction perception. "Accuracy" can be estimated by comparing teacher and student perceptions with observed frequencies. While observer records are not objective reality, they do represent a third party's interpretation of classroom events. Although such comparisons are not as directly pertinent to the model as those in Study I, the question of accuracy may substantiate old insights or provide new insights into the expectation communication process.

Teacher Awareness of Classroom Behavior.   Past research indicates that teachers and classroom observers often disagree about what has occurred in a classroom (Hook and Rosenshine, 1979). For instance, Squire and Applebee (1966) found that high school English teachers reported using class discussion and Socratic questioning much more frequently than noted by observers. Similarly, Goodlad and associates (1970) found that teachers claimed to engage in behaviors that classroom observers found absent. Ehman (Note 7.1) asked social studies teachers to estimate how free their students were to express their opinions. Teacher reports were compared with observers who recorded (1) the student-to-teacher talk ratio and (2) the student-initiated-to-teacher-initiated student talk ratio. Ehman found a *negative* correlation between these observational measures and teacher reports. Finally, Good and Brophy (1974) found that teachers were considerably better at describing the quantity than quality of interactions with particular students; however, some teachers were poor estimators of both.

Two reasons have been given for why teachers may not be aware of many aspects of classroom behavior: (1) there are too many interactions during an instructional day for teachers to process (Jackson, 1968; Rohrkemper, 1982) and (2) teachers deal with too many students to accurately associate events with individuals. Whatever the reason, it appears teachers are often not cognizant of their behavior, *if* classroom-observer descriptions are taken as veridical.

Student Awareness of Classroom Behavior.   Two previous attempts to assess the accuracy of student reports of classroom behavior were found.

First, the Ehman (Note 7.1) study reported above also asked students how free they felt they were to express their opinions in class. Ehman found moderate positive relations between these reports and the two corresponding observational measures. Second, Gustafsson (1977) asked students whether they received more or less questions and more or less individual assistance from their teacher than did other students. She notes that there was absolutely no correspondence between these answers and the students' actual classroom behavior. About 85 percent of the pupils chose the middle alternative, demonstrating their reluctance to suggest they differed from other students.

The paucity of data on student awareness makes it difficult to draw firm conclusions about the correspondence between observational records and student perceptions. The present study is intended to provide new evidence on this question.

Method

Interaction Frequency Perceptions. The same interaction frequency perceptions used in Study I were again used in Study II.

Observed Interaction Frequencies. The behavior observations corresponding to each interaction frequency perception are described in Chapter 2 and listed with perceptions in Study I.

Data Analysis Strategy. For each of the nine behaviors separately, the students in each class were grouped according to whether their observed frequency of the behavior was above or below the class average. These groupings were then used as the independent variables in one-way analyses of variance. Above versus below classmate's frequency was treated as a repeated measurement on the classroom unit. Dependent variables for each behavior were the corresponding teacher and student perceptions of the frequency of the behavior. For instance, teacher and student perceptions of the frequency of teacher initiations in public were analyzed in separate one-way ANOVAs. In both ANOVAs the perceptions were compared for students whose observed frequency of teacher initiations in public was above versus below the class average. For one behavior, absolute criticism, the observed frequency was too low to reliably classify students, so this behavior was not analyzed.

A second set of analyses was conducted to compare teacher and student perceptions directly. Here, teacher perceptions were used as the "independent" variable and student perceptions as the dependent variable. Students in each class were grouped according to whether the teacher reported the student's occurrence of each interaction as being above, about the same as, or below the class average. One-way three-group ANOVAs were then performed on student perceptions of the same behavior.

Results

Perceived and Observed Frequencies. The means presented in Tables 7.5 and 7.6 pertain to the correspondence between (1) observers' records of classroom interaction occurring in the spring and (2) the perceptions of teachers and students collected at about the same time.

Teachers' beliefs about interactions corresponded closely with observed frequencies for many behaviors (Table 7.5). Specifically, teachers "accurately" discriminated between students who received high- and low-interaction frequencies in the following categories: teacher-initiated public interactions $[F (1, 14) = 41.00, p < .001]$; teacher-initiated private interactions $[F (1, 14) = 10.18, p < .006]$; student-initiated public interactions $[F (1, 14) = 45.87, p < .001]$; student-initiated private interactions $[F (1, 14) = 16.18, p < .002]$; no teacher evaluation following student response $[F (1, 14) = 7.66, p < .02]$; and behavior interventions $[F (1, 14) = 24.96, p < .001]$. Teachers' judgments about who provided the greatest number of appropriate responses also approached significance $[F (1, 14) = 3.0, p < .10]$. The remaining behavior, absolute praise, revealed no difference and almost equal means across conditions.

In contrast, students' discriminations of classroom events (Table 7.6) matched those of observational records only on the behavioral intervention category $[F (1, 14) = 57.01, p < .01]$. All student means were in the "accurate" direction, however.

Congruence Between Teacher and Student Perceptions. Table 7.7 presents the correspondence between teacher and student beliefs about classroom interaction frequencies. In the table, students were divided into three groups on the basis of teacher reports. The classification of students was done separately for each variable.

Table 7.7 reveals a general correspondence between teacher beliefs and student beliefs. There was significant agreement between teachers and students about (1) who received the most teacher questions in public $[F (1, 41) = 7.25, p < .002]$; (2) who created the most student-initiated private contacts with teachers $[F (1, 40) = 6.50, p < .004]$; (3) who answered the most teacher questions appropriately $[F (1, 44) = 4.10, p < .03]$; (4) who failed to receive evaluation following their answers most frequently $[F (1, 26) = 9.93, p < .001]$; and (5) who received the most behavior interventions from teachers $[F (1, 44) = 21.67, p < .001]$.

Discussion

Previous research has described teachers as being poor reporters of classroom events. However, the data collected in the present study showed

TABLE 7.5 Comparison of Observed Interaction Frequencies with Teacher Perceptions

Interaction Perceptions of Teachers	Students With		F test	p value
	Observed Low Frequencies	Observed High Frequencies		
Teacher-initiated public interaction	1.70	2.15	41.00	.001
Teacher-initiated private interaction	1.84	2.12	10.18	.006
Student-initiated public interaction	1.59	2.18	45.87	.001
Student-initiated private interaction	1.54	1.89	16.18	.002
Number of appropriate responses	1.96	2.18	3.00	.10
Absolute amount of praise	2.09	2.10	.03	...
No teacher evaluation following student response	1.74	1.94	7.66	.02
Behavioral intervention	1.65	2.23	24.96	.001

TABLE 7.6 Comparison of Observed Interaction Frequencies with Student Perceptions

Interaction Perceptions of Students	Students With		F test	p value
	Observed Low Frequencies	Observed High Frequencies		
Teacher-initiated public interaction	3.42	3.59	1.04	...
Teacher-initiated private interaction	3.12	3.27	1.20	...
Student-initiated public interaction	1.54	1.54	.00	...
Student-initiated private interaction	1.68	1.81	2.26	.15
Number of appropriate responses	4.00	4.23	2.45	.14
Absolute amount of praise	3.78	3.80	.00	...
No teacher evaluation following student response	1.60	1.73	1.41	...
Behavioral intervention	2.82	3.93	57.01	.001

TABLE 7.7 Comparison of Teachers' Perceptions of Classroom Interaction Rates with those of Students

Interaction Perceptions of Students	Students Described by Teachers as Engaging in the Interaction			F	P
	Most Frequently	About Average	Least Frequently		
Teacher-initiated public interaction	3.8	3.6	2.9	7.25	.002
Teacher-initiated private interaction	3.5	3.2	3.0	1.76	...
Student-initiated public interaction	1.5	1.5	1.5	.02	...
Student-initiated private interaction	2.1	1.8	1.5	6.50	.004
Number of appropriate answers	.4	3.9	3.9	4.10	.03
Absolute number of praise	3.5	3.9	3.4	2.05	.14
No teacher evaluation following student response	2.4	1.7	1.4	9.93	.001
Behavioral intervention	.3	3.2	2.9	21.67	.001
Absolute amount of teacher criticism	3.2	3.2	3.0	.30	...

that teachers in general were aware of the actual interaction differences they had with individual students. The inconsistency between the present result and past research may lie in the way interactions were defined. The present study defined interactions in operational terms (i.e., number of public and private interactions, etc.) whereas most previous research defined interactions more globally and conceptually (i.e., use of "discussion," "freeness" to express opinions). Thus, this study probably contained considerable agreement about definitions between teachers and observers whereas previous research may have been hampered by definitional ambiguity.

It is interesting that the behavior which produced the least correspondence between teacher perceptions and observations was praise. This result should not be surprising since it is the same behavior about which teachers proved least aware of expectation differences. These results invite further careful scrutiny of the phenomenology of positive reinforcement. It is regrettable that the present study could only frame the question and offer speculations about some possible answers. Future research must examine the different functions of praise in classrooms (Brophy, 1981) as well as (1) whether teacher reports of praise are affected by self-presentation concerns and (2) whether teachers are differentially aware of use of praise with different students.

Students were also generally "accurate" in estimating how frequently particular classroom events occurred for them. They did not, however, demonstrate nearly the same degree of "accuracy" as teachers. There are several reasons why this may be the case. First, as we have noted previously, the language of the questionnaire may have been appropriate for teachers but inappropriate for students. That is, definitions that the students assigned to terms may vary greatly from student to student and may also be discrepant with meanings that researchers attach to the terms.

Second, the time between the collection of observational data and students' responses to the questionnaire may have been too great. It would be instructional to have students fill out the questionnaire on the actual day of observation and ask questions that pertain exclusively to that day. Student perceptions may be more "accurate" in a more immediate time frame than they are over a longer period of time.

A third source of inaccuracy in student recall of classroom behavior may have been a tendency to over- or underreport certain interaction patterns with the teachers for social desirability reasons. As noted earlier, Gustafsson (1977) found students were very reluctant to admit that they got more or fewer questions or more or less individual assistance from the teacher than did other students. For example, in interviews with a few pupils following the questionnaire collection, pupils made comments such as, "Miss X does as good as she can. She comes to all of us."

Finally, students were asked to estimate the frequency with which events occurred for them relative to classmates. Thus, students were asked not only to recall their personal frequencies but also to estimate the frequency of others. Teachers should be more accurate in making these relative judgments because they took part in all interactions, while students may be only partially aware of how many times interactions occur for peers.

Given these obstacles, it is encouraging that students displayed even marginal accuracy in perceptions and not surprising that teachers were more accurate than students. The study of what students see and remember in the classroom is important. However, it is a fledgling research area and like all beginning research paradigms, it needs much developmental work. Basic information about ways to ask students to compare themselves with other students must be explored. Also needed are better ways to measure student perceptions of variations in instructional behavior (see for example, Koopman and Newtson, 1981).

The symmetry in teacher and student perceptions of interactions is difficult to evaluate because each measurement is affected by the separate sources of inaccuracy described above. Perhaps most notable was the almost total lack of congruence between teacher and student perceptions of teacher use of praise and criticism. If these findings are not completely due to methodological problems, they may demonstrate a considerable degree of miscommunication in the classroom.

8

Student Beliefs about Academic Self-Efficacy

Chapter Overview

Chapter 8 contains three studies involving student beliefs about the role of effort in academic outcomes. In Study I, teacher expectations, student gender, grade level, and time of the school year are used to predict student responses on an effort-related subscale of the Intellectual-Achievement Responsibility (IAR) Scale. Congruent with the communication model, high-expectation students were found to have generally stronger beliefs than low-expectation students that effort and outcome covaried. Girls also tended to have stronger self-efficacy beliefs than did boys. In Study II, the self-efficacy beliefs measured by the IAR scale were correlated with the different classroom interaction frequencies. The most support for the Expectation Communication Model was found for within-class relations early in the school year: the model correctly predicted the direction of nine of ten tested relations. Finally, Study III related student self-efficacy beliefs to student perceptions of the frequency of interactions with teachers. These results were generally not supportive of the model, but several design problems are discussed which might explain the findings.

Student Self-Efficacy Beliefs

In previous chapters, several pieces of evidence were presented which suggested that teachers' reinforcement contingencies and teacher-pupil initiation rates vary according to characteristics of students. Teachers were found to give more control-related feedback to low-expectation students (Chapter 6), low-expectation students sought and received fewer exchanges with the teacher (Chapter 4), and both high- and low-achieving students were aware of the teaching behavior they received (Chapter 7). To complete the Expectation Communication Model, we must next ask whether these behavioral differences are associated with the way students think about themselves and their role in the classroom. Unless such links can be demonstrated, the expectation communication process would be "short-circuited." No matter how discrepant teacher behaviors are toward different students, if students do not incorporate this treatment into their self-perceptions it makes little sense to argue that teacher behavior differences influence student effort or motivation.

For present purposes, the student self-perception of primary interest can be labeled self-efficacy (see Bandura, 1977). This perception involves the degree to which the student believes that trying hard will produce positive academic outcomes. A strong belief in effort-outcome covariation is an important antecedent to achievement motivation. In support of this notion, Kukla (1972) found that people who were highest in achievement motivation also had the strongest belief that hard work pays off.

At least two explanations can be offered for the proposed cognition-motivation relation. The first involves a simple logical deduction on the part of the student. That is, if a student does not believe that hard work pays off, the student has little reason to display motivated behavior. Like any reinforcement process, if effort is not systematically rewarded through positive outcomes and praise from the teacher, effort-related behavior is likely to disappear. Of course, this proposition is stated in an all-or-none fashion, but it would be true in degrees as well: a lesser effort contingency to reward means less effortful behavior.

The second explanation for the relation between self-efficacy beliefs and achievement motivation involves the student's potential affective responses to success and failure outcomes (Phares, 1976). Apparently, the attribution of success to one's own effort leads to the most positive affective reactions, while failures attributed to lack of effort generate the most negative feelings. For instance, Weiner, Russell, and Lerman (1978) found that people who attributed success to effort described their emotions as "uproarious," "delirious," and "delighted." When failure was attributed to lack of effort, the dominant affective reactions were "shame" and "guilt." Other attributions led to reactions which were not nearly this extreme. Clearly, the student who believes strongly in effort-outcome covariation has good reason to work hard for success. For these students, the internal affective rewards for success and punishments for failure may be considerably more potent than those experienced by students with weak effort-outcome covariation beliefs.

These principles, relating cognitions and emotions, can be readily applied to teacher-expectation phenomena. If high-expectation students are more likely than low-expectation students to perceive that effort deter-mines their reinforcements, it should not be surprising to find that they also exhibit greater motivation for achievement.

The Present Studies

Three studies will be reported which examined the relations between teacher expectations, student efficacy beliefs, and classroom interactions. In the first study, the hypothesis that student efficacy beliefs are positively related to teacher expectations was tested. In Study II, the relations be-tween student efficacy beliefs and the frequencies of observed classroom interactions were examined. Finally, in Study III efficacy beliefs were related to student *perceptions* of the frequency of classroom interactions.

The three studies covered the final links in the Expectation Com-munication Model tested in this project. They do not represent the final links in the expectation communication process, however. Student differ-ences in self-efficacy beliefs must be shown to affect achievement motiva-tion, and achievement motivation, in turn, must influence actual achieve-ment. In an extensive review of the literature concerning the motivational antecedents of achievement, Uguroglu and Walberg (1979) found indirect support for these last notions. They reported that locus of control was found to correlate with achievement +.32 on the average in thirteen stud-ies, and achievement motivation correlated with achievement +.31 on the average. While locus of control is not synonymous with student self-efficacy beliefs, these concepts are certainly highly related.

STUDY I.   TEACHER EXPECTATIONS AND STUDENT EFFICACY BELIEFS

The Expectation Communication Model makes the prediction that students for whom teachers hold high expectations should perceive a stronger effort contingency for rewards than low-expectation students. As discussed in Chapter 1 and demonstrated in Chapter 6, the basis of this difference in beliefs may be an objective difference in the amount of effort-contingent reinforcement the two groups of students receive. Low-expectation students' reinforcements may more often depend on the teacher's desire for future interactions with lows to occur in controllable settings. Since controlling high-expectation students' behavior is not an issue, some teachers may more often employ reinforcement to reflect ple-asure or dissatisfaction with high students' effort, rather than as a class-room-management device.

Gender.   In addition to teacher expectations, Study I also examined the relation of student gender to self-efficacy beliefs. It was predicted that females would express stronger self-efficacy beliefs than would males. This prediction was based on two previous research findings. First, teachers tend to express generally higher expectations for girls than for boys and these differences are reflected in the children's self-expectations (Entwisle and Hayduk, 1978). To the extent that gender and expectations are confounded, we would predict that gender is the "spurious" variable, while expectations is the "true" causal operator on beliefs. Second, girls appear to conform more closely than do boys to teachers' perceptions of what the "ideal" elementary school child should be (Feshbach, 1969). If this is the case, then controlling or directing boys' behavior is probably a more important goal of teachers than is controlling girls' behavior (Brophy and Good, 1974). It was expected, then, that reinforcements to boys are more often meant to control boys' behavior. As a consequence, we would expect boys to perceive their own efforts as less often causing their reinforcements. This prediction is in contrast to the thinking of Dweck and colleagues (cf. Dweck and Reppucci, 1973; Dweck, Davidson, Nelson, and Enna, 1978; Dweck, Goetz, and Strauss, 1980). Readers interested in the gender differences are referred to Cooper, Burger, and Good (1981) for a more thorough discussion of this topic. The Cooper et al. (1981) paper emphasized an attributional analysis of the gender difference rather than an expectation analysis.

Grade. Based on findings related to general locus of control beliefs, it was also predicted that self-efficacy beliefs would be stronger for students in later grades. For instance, Crandall, Katkovsky, and Crandall (1965) found that students' locus of control beliefs became increasingly internal from the third through the eleventh grade. As with gender, the grade (or age) variable probably does not cause greater self-efficacy beliefs. Rather, grade probably serves as a proxy for other developmental phenomena, such as increasing verbal fluency (Brechner and Denmark, 1969) and increasing social responsibilities.

Time of Year. Finally, it was anticipated that the time of the school year when beliefs were measured would also show the developmental effects. Specifically, self-efficacy beliefs were predicted to be stronger at the end of the school year than at the beginning.

Method

Self-Efficacy Measure. Approximately one month into the school year, and again approximately one month before the end of the school year, each of the target students completed the Intellectual Achievement Responsibility (IAR) Questionnaire (Crandall, Katkovsky, and Crandall,

1965). The IAR consists of thirty-four forced-choice items which ask the student to select the alternative which best explains the occurrence of success and failure at academic tasks. For example, one question asks, "When you do well on a test at school, is it more likely to be (*a*) because you studied for it or (*b*) because the test was especially easy?" Each item presents one internal causal explanation and one external explanation. Responses can be summed (+1 = internal response, 0 = external response) to form a total scale score or separate subscales for success and failure. For the present study, an effort or self-efficacy scale was created by summing all items whose internal response implied that personal *effort* was the cause of either success or failure.

The IAR was administered to each classroom as a group by two experimenters. An experimenter read each item aloud as the students filled out the questionnaires. A second experimenter was present during each administration to help answer any questions and to monitor the classroom. Experimenter pairs varied in gender composition but usually contained one male and one female.

Of the thirty-two IAR items, sixteen included internal explanations related to students' effort. These sixteen items were summed to form a single scale. The items involved were 2, 3, 6, 8, 9, 11, 12, 14, 15, 16, 19, 23, 25, 28, 29, and 33. Thus, students could have a score from 0 to 16, with 16 meaning that they always chose the effort cause.

Other Variables. The level of expectation (high/average/low), gender, grade (third/fourth/fifth), and time of school year (fall/spring) variables were all defined as described in Chapter 2.

Analytic Design. The ANOVA model presented in Chapter 3 was employed. Each classroom was conceptualized as the unit of analysis with teacher expectation, student gender, and time of school year treated as within-class crossed conditions. Grade level was treated as a between-classrooms factor.

Results

Expectations. The analysis of variance produced no significant effects associated with teacher-expectation level. An examination of the direction of means, however, did reveal the predicted pattern: self-efficacy beliefs were positively related to teacher expectations (high expectations, M = 11.42; average expectations, M = 11.14; low expectations, M = 10.88).

Gender and Grade Level. A two-way interaction involving student gender and grade level approached significance [$F(2, 13) = 3.11$, $p < .09$]. The relevant means appear in Table 8.1. A Newman-Keuls post-hoc means

TABLE 8.1   Student Self-Efficacy Beliefs for Each Student Gender and Grade Level

| | Gender | |
Grade	Male	Female
Third	10.94b	10.80b
Fourth	10.67*b*	11.41ab
Fifth	11.31ab	11.95a

Note. Means not sharing subscripts differed significantly by the Newman-Keuls test ($p <$ .05).

test revealed fifth-grade girls had stronger self-efficacy beliefs than did third-grade boys and girls and fourth-grade boys (p. $<$ .05). No other means differed significantly.

Time of Year. No time-of-year effects reached or approached significance.

Discussion

Although the direction of results in this study were consistent with the a priori predictions, the strength of the results were extremely weak. None of the predicted relations reached significance. There are several potential reasons why the relation between teacher expectations and student self-efficacy beliefs was not strong. From a theoretical perspective, teacher expectations and student efficacy beliefs are the most distant concepts in the model. Many variables are suggested as mediating their relation. On this basis, only a weak correspondence between the two might be anticipated. A second explanation involves measurement. The subscale of the IAR used to measure self-efficacy beliefs contained only sixteen questions involving many diverse academic tasks. This instrument may have been too insensitive to uncover the subtle relation. Finally, as discussed in Chapter 3, the conservative choice of unit of analysis (the classroom) made it difficult for all but the strongest effects to reach significance. Thus, while a more robust finding would have been desirable, we must bear in mind that (1) the uncovered means were consistent with predictions and (2) many elements of the research design worked against finding a strong relation. This leads to the conclusions that the results should not be viewed as discouraging and the predictions deserve a better test.

The measurement and unit-of-analysis difficulties described above also pertain to the general failure to find gender and developmental effects (although here a gender by grade interaction did emerge). Gender effects might also have been mitigated by the selection procedures (described in Chapter 2) which chose boys and girls from within expectation groups (see Chapter 4). It should also be pointed out that gender and grade means were again in the direction predicted by the model and past research.

STUDY II. STUDENT-EFFICACY BELIEFS AND CLASSROOM BEHAVIOR

The first study of student self-efficacy beliefs dealt with variables separated by many mediators in the communication process. Study II shortens the causal chain of variables by replacing teacher expectations with interactive behaviors as the determinants of student cognitions.

Teacher Feedback. The central test of the Expectation Communication Model in Study II involves teacher feedback. The model predicts that low-expectations students will be criticized by the teacher more often than high-expectation students and that highs will receive more praise. This strategy is invoked by the teacher in order to inhibit lows from initiating interactions. It is also proposed that because of the teacher's concern with controlling interactions, the feedback received by lows will be less contingent on their efforts than the feedback received by highs. If these relations hold, then the following hypotheses for Study II can be offered:

1. Students who receive more criticism relative to their classmates should perceive less self-efficacy. Likewise, more instances of teachers' ignoring a student's responses should be associated with weaker self-efficacy beliefs (if we again assume that ignoring responses is akin to mildly negative feedback).
2. Students who receive more praise than classmates should perceive more self-efficacy.
3. Students who perceive more self-efficacy than classmates should initiate more interactions with the teacher.

In predictions 1 and 2, student efficacy beliefs are the dependent variables (i.e., teacher feedback causes student beliefs). The third prediction views the student efficacy belief as the causal agent. That is, a strong covariation belief by the student is proposed to lead to more initiation of interaction with the teacher. While these are the proposed causal sequences, the present data were associational in nature. Therefore, the proposed direction of relations can be tested, but not the causal sequence of effect.

No difference in relations was predicted for the between- and within-class levels of analyses. The hypotheses were stated at the within-class level, but they can be recast as between-class statements as well. For instance, in classes where more criticism is employed, students should report weaker self-efficacy beliefs. Although the theoretical model makes no distinction between levels of analysis, the earlier empirical findings would probably lead to a prediction that the results most supportive of the hypotheses would be obtained from within-class processes early in the school year.

The three hypotheses of Study II have gained empirical support from an earlier investigation. Cooper (1977) found that higher IAR effort scores were associated with more student initiations and less teacher criticism following these initiations. However, Cooper used residualized student scores as the unit of analysis, so the significance levels associated with this finding are somewhat suspect (see Chapter 3).

Interaction Frequencies. It was also possible to make some ancillary predictions regarding the frequency of teacher-student interactions. For instance, it could be expected that students who more often responded appropriately would also report stronger self-efficacy beliefs. This prediction is based on the observation that high-expectation students get more things right and fewer things wrong. Similarly, since low-expectation students display more problem behaviors, it could be predicted that the frequency of teacher reprimands should be negatively related to student efficacy beliefs. Finally, teachers should prefer to call on students whom they expect will try hard, especially in situations which afford the teacher least control (i.e., public). Therefore, it could be predicted that a positive relation would exist between the frequency of teacher initiations in public and the student's efficacy belief, while a negative relation might exist between teacher-private initiations and student covariation beliefs.

Method

Self-Efficacy Measure. The IAR effort subscale scores for each student used in Study I were used in Study II as well.

Observed Behaviors. The behavior frequencies used in these analyses were as follows:

1. Teacher-initiated public interactions
2. Student-initiated public interactions
3. Teacher-initiated private interactions
4. Student-initiated private interactions
5. Correct or appropriate responses
6. Incorrect or inappropriate responses
7. Relative praise
8. Relative no feedback

9. Relative criticism
10. Behavioral interventions

More detailed descriptions of the behavioral categories and how scores were formed can be found in Chapter 2.

Since IAR effort scores were collected in fall and spring only, the winter behavior observations were not used in this experiment.

Analytic Strategy. The correlational approach to analytic-level specification (described in Chapter 3) was used in this study. Briefly, for between-classroom analyses, the average efficacy belief and the average behavior frequency for each class were paired and correlated. Significant correlations indicate that a greater than zero relation exists when differences in classrooms are at issue. For within-classroom analyses, students' IAR effort scores were paired individually with their behavior frequency scores and a correlation between the two measures was computed for each classroom. The correlations were then transformed to Z scores and a t test was employed to determine whether the sample of correlations differed significantly from zero. Because teacher criticism was never observed in some classrooms, only eight within-class correlations were available for criticism analyses. No evaluation occurred in fifteen classrooms in September and thirteen in May.

TABLE 8.2   Relations of Student Self-Efficacy Beliefs and the Frequency of Classroom Interactions

Student Effort-Outcome Covariation Beliefs and Frequency of	Between-Classrooms Correlations		Within-Classrooms Average Correlation	
	Fall	Spring	Fall	Spring
Teacher initiations in public	+.37a	+.38a	+.13c	+.09
Teacher initiations in private	+.12	−.04	−.12c	+.04
Student initiations in public	−.23	+.18	+.07	−.01
Student initiations in private	−.05	−.22	−.02	+.08
Appropriate responses	+.28	+.37a	+.11b	+.09
Inappropriate responses	+.25	+.20	−.01	+.04
Praise following an appropriate response	−.00	−.22	−.01	+.05
Criticism following an inappropriate response	−.26	−.56	−.11	+.07
No evaluation following any response	−.11	+.06	−.07	+.02
Teacher behavioral interventions	+.23	−.22	−.08	+.04

a. $p < .16$
b. $p < .08$
c. $p < .05$

Results

Between-Class Relations. Table 8.2 presents the correlations between the average frequency of the ten classroom interactions and the students' average IAR effort scores. Correlations are presented separately for fall and spring.

In fall, no between-class relation reached or approached significance. However, one relation produced consistent moderate-sized relations in both spring and fall: In classrooms where teachers initiated more public interaction, the students reported stronger efficacy beliefs: for fall [$\bar{r}$ (16) = +.37, $p < .16$]; for spring [$\bar{r}$ (16) = +.38, $p < .16$]. At the end of the year there was one notable association which was not present in fall. Classrooms with the more criticism per interaction showed weaker average student efficacy beliefs [$\bar{r}$ (15) = +.56, $p < .05$]. Whereas the fall result ($\bar{r}$ = +.26) was not nearly as strong as the spring result, the direction of this relation was consistent at both times of the school year.

Within-Class Relations. Table 8.2 also presents the average correlations found in the within-classroom analyses. The fall results produced evidence of a positive relation between the teachers' frequency of academic initiations and the students' efficacy beliefs. At the beginning of the school year, teacher initiations in public were positively related to IAR effort scores [$\bar{r}$ = +.13, t (15) = 2.33, $p < .04$]. More frequent public initiation by the teacher was associated with stronger student efficacy beliefs relative to other classmates. In addition, students participating in more frequent private exchanges initiated by the teacher were found to have lower IAR effort scores [$\bar{r}$ = −.12, t (16) = 2.38, $p < .04$]. In fall, then, teacher-initiation differences toward classmates were related to student efficacy beliefs in ways predicted by the Expectation Communication Model. Also as predicted (but this time by previous results) the data supported the model more strongly in fall than spring. The end-of-year data revealed no notable relations between IAR effort scores and the frequency of academic exchanges.

One final result worth noting was that students who gave more frequent appropriate responses also tended to report greater self-efficacy beliefs relative to classmates. In fall, this relation was nearly significant [$\bar{r}$ = +.11, t (16) = 2.00, $p < .08$], but it did not approach significance in the spring ($\bar{r}$ = + .09).

Discussion

Study II produced partial support for the Expectation Communication Model. The model correctly predicted nine of the ten directions for within-in-class relations at the beginning of the school year, although only two of these reached significance (teacher initiations in public and private) and one approached significance (appropriate responses). The model was much less effective at predicting relations in spring or between classrooms. The model was predictive of only three relations within classrooms at year's end. At the between-classrooms level, the model predicted five relational directions in fall and seven in spring.

The fall within-class data involving academic exchanges produced the most reliable statistical findings. The interaction setting (public vs. private) was a strong mediator of whether the frequency of interaction and IAR effort scores were positively or negatively related. Students with strong efficacy beliefs interacted with teachers in public situations more often than students with weak self-efficacy beliefs, while weak self-efficacy believers interacted with teachers more often in private. These relations were predicted by the model. Teachers probably choose strong self-efficacy believers to talk in front of others more often because they are more controllable individuals in the more uncontrolled (public) situation. The less controllable individuals are interacted with more frequently in the more controlled (private) situation. The model was also able to predict to some degree the negative relations of criticism and no evaluation to IAR effort scores for the within-classroom fall data set, though these results were not statistically reliable.

The present study was thus a generally successful replication of Cooper's (1977) investigation and it provided some support for the Expectation Communication Model. The earlier study was conducted with no attention paid to issues of unit of analysis or time of year. However, Cooper's (1977) choices about timing (fall) and unit (student scores residualized by their class means) appear to have been exactly those needed to constrain the data set so as to produce findings which confirmed the model. According to the present study, had Cooper (1977) chosen to run the investigation in spring rather than fall, he might have reached an entirely different conclusion about the model's validity.

The between-classrooms analyses revealed two relations which apparently have some temporal stability. Both relations were in the direction predicted by the model. Specifically, students felt greater self-efficacy in classrooms where (1) teachers more frequently initiated public exchanges and (2) criticism was used less often. Our interest in claiming that these results are a strong confirmation of the model is tempered by the relatively poor ability of the model to predict the direction of nonsignificant relations. Of the eight nonsignificant relations, three were in the direction predicted by the model in fall and five in spring.

STUDY III. STUDENT EFFICACY BELIEFS AND BEHAVIOR PERCEPTIONS

In Chapter 7 teachers were found to be quite accurate in grouping students according to their relative frequency of dyadic interaction with the teacher. Students, however, were somewhat less able to accurately group themselves according to their interaction with their teacher. Students who were observed to engage in a particular interaction with the teacher more frequently than their classmates differed only slightly from their classmates in their *perception* of where they stood in the frequency distribution. Ideally, a great deal of similarity should exist between actual and student-perceived frequency differences. Since this was not the case, however, the question of which data set best fits the model is a meaningful one.

As originally presented, the Expectation Communication Model (Chapter 1) focused on the actual observed behavior differences between teacher-student dyads and not on the student's perception of these differences. Use of the same causal-sequencing logic with which the model was developed, however, means that perceptions of behavior might intervene between actual behaviors and self-efficacy beliefs. We would expect, then, that the behavior perceptions would relate to efficacy beliefs in the same manner predicted for the actual behaviors, and perhaps would reveal even stronger correlations. Therefore, the same predictions made in Study II for observed frequencies of behavior were made in Study III for perceived frequencies.

The results of Study III, however, have some design limitations that require that they be interpreted cautiously. First, only within-class relations could be tested. Students were asked to compare themselves only with their classmates with regard to the frequency with which an interaction occurred (see Chapter 7). Students were not asked to compare their class to other classes. Second, behavior perceptions were gathered only at the end of the school year. Thus, the relations of behavior perceptions to self-efficacy beliefs in fall could not be tested. In Study II the most support for the model was present early in the school year. It might therefore be more surprising if Study III found support for the model in spring than if no support was found. To obtain some limited information on the fall relations, the end-of-year behavior perceptions were related to the start-of-year IAR effort scores. Temporally, this sequence is opposite to that being predicted (i.e., earlier behavior perceptions influence later IAR effort scores). However, if the students' spring behavior perceptions are a culmination of the entire year's interactions with the teacher, then this analysis may have some validity: we would expect beginning and end-of-year perceptions to be positively correlated. However, because interaction frequencies and cognition-behavior relations have been found to change dramatically over the course of the year, the use of late beliefs as a proxy for early beliefs must be viewed cautiously.

Method

Self-Efficacy Measure. The same IAR effort scores used for students in Studies I and II were used in Study III.

Behavior Perception Measures. The behavior perception measures used in Chapter 7 were used here as well. Student perceptions of the relative frequency of nine interactions with the teacher were gathered. These are presented in Table 3. The behaviors were:

1. Teacher initiations in public
2. Teacher initiations in private
3. Student initiations in public
4. Student initiations in private
5. Appropriate responses
6. Absolute praise
7. Absolute criticism
8. Absolute no evaluation
9. Behavioral interventions

Analytic Design. The ANOVA model described in Chapter 3 was used. Students in each class were grouped according to whether they believed their personal frequency of each behavior was more than, about the same as, or less than classmates. Students were grouped independently for each behavior and the average IAR effort score for each group was computed. Separate analyses were conducted for fall and spring. The three average IAR effort scores were then placed into a one-factor (more/same/less), repeated-measures analysis of variance, with classroom as the unit of repeated observation. For those behaviors about which two questions were asked (see Chapter 7), the responses were coded 1 for less than, 2 for about the same as, and 3 for more than other students and then responses were summed. If the students scored a 2 or 3, they were placed in the less than group; if they scored a 4, they were placed in the about the same as group; and if they scored a 5 or 6 they were placed in the more than group. The analysis of variance was then conducted as above.

Results

Table 8.3 presents the mean IAR effort score for each of the three relative frequencies of each behavior. Only three of the eighteen analyses of variance produced results even approaching statistical significance. In fall, students who perceived themselves as receiving more praise from the teacher tended to report stronger self-efficacy beliefs [$F (2, 29) = 2.47, p$

TABLE 8.3 Student Self-Efficacy Beliefs for Each Perceived Frequency of Different Interactions at Different Times of the School Year

| | Perceived Frequency of Interaction Relative to Other Students | | | | | | | |
| | Fall | | | | Spring | | | |
Type of Interaction	More	Same	Less	p Level	More	Same	Less	p Level
Teacher initiations in public	11.6	12.1	11.2	.15	10.4	12.4	11.6	.04
Teacher initiations in private	11.8	11.5	11.4	...	11.9	11.9	11.6	...
Student initiations in public	12.0	12.0	11.3	...	11.6	11.7	11.8	...
Student initiations in private	11.5	11.4	11.8	...	11.8	11.8	11.4	...
Teacher behavioral interventions	11.7	11.8	11.6	...	11.9	11.6	11.7	...
Appropriate responses	10.7	11.7	11.7	...	10.7	12.0	11.8	.08
Praise following an appropriate response	12.2	11.8	10.7	.11	11.8	11.9	11.5	...
Criticism following an inappropriate response	10.6	11.5	11.7	...	10.9	11.9	11.7	...
No evaluation following any response	11.3	11.4	11.4	...	12.2	11.4	11.9	...

< .11]. In spring, the perceived frequency of teacher initiations was related to IAR effort scores [F (2, 25) = 3.78, p < .04], but apparently not in a linear fashion. Students perceiving no difference in this frequency between themselves and their classmates had the highest IAR effort scores. Students perceiving the most frequent teacher initiations in public had the lowest IAR effort scores. Finally, the students' perceived frequency of appropriate responding and self-efficacy beliefs tended to be related [F (2, 29) = 2.81, p < .08]. Apparently, students who felt they more often responded appropriately reported weaker covariation beliefs.

Discussion

The results of Study III showed little replication of Study II findings. The only encouraging note was that the three relations between student perception of the teachers' use of feedback and student self-efficacy beliefs were in the direction predicted by the model in fall. In spring, little support for the model was found.

There are many possible reasons for the general failure to uncover significant relations in this data set. One reason, that measures of behavior perceptions were taken only in spring, was mentioned earlier. Also, it might be that too few questions (one or two) were asked on each behavior. Undoubtedly, these measures contained a substantial amount of error, thus obscuring potential relations. Finally, the social desirability of certain responses might have played a role in these results. Students may not wish to acknowledge that their frequency of appropriate responding or initiation is below that of classmates.

Though this particular effort to relate classroom behavior perceptions to self-efficacy beliefs was not very successful, it should not be concluded that behavior perceptions do not mediate the Expectation Communication Process. We prefer to think of Study III as a pilot study which has helped identify some of the design parameters that need attention before a better test of the mediation hypothesis can be undertaken. The results of such research will help to determine the extent to which students' behavior perceptions mediate the Expectation Communication Process.

Part III

Summary and Conclusion

9

Modifications in the Model and Future Research

Chapter Overview

Chapter 9 first addresses modifications in the theoretical model which were suggested by the data. The revisions fall into two general categories: (1) changes in model constructs and (2) restrictions on the model's generality. First, the notion of control is redefined to involve two control referents, each salient under separate conditions. Second, the role of attribution-feedback relations is reexamined to incorporate into the model the uncovered association between teacher involvement and reinforcement. Next, student perceptions of teachers and teacher behavior are given important roles in the expectation communication process. Finally, three distinctions are offered which may affect the model's applicability: (1) the decision of whether between- or within-classroom relations are at issue, (2) the time of the school year, and (3) the social class of the students under study.

Chapter 9 closes with a discussion of needed future research. Other teacher and student cognitions are suggested that might help explain expectation communication. Some important questions that longitudinal research can address (both within and across school years) are also examined.

Three Years of Research

Three years have passed since the Expectation Communication Model was first presented (Cooper, 1979). The first year was spent developing instruments needed to measure variables central to the model. The second year involved collecting model-generated data. Nearly 500 individual data points were collected on over 200 students. The third year was spent struggling with data analysis, trying to reduce data in a meaningful conceptual fashion, and interpreting data patterns. At each stage of research, the goal of integrating social theory with a practical educational problem created "trade-offs." A decision to protect the naturalistic nature of the study often seemed to confuse some important conceptual issue. A decision to maintain the theoretical purity of the study sometimes reduced the data's relevance to ongoing classrooms. Decisions regarding legal issues (informed consent, rights of privacy) often seemed to reduce both theoretical and practical relevance.

The past 3 years have provided information about the model in addition to the formal data analysis. The participating teachers and classroom coders made valuable comments on every aspect of the model and design of the study. Teachers' views were given particular attention because their perspective is distinct from that of theorists and data analysts. Also, other researchers have had an opportunity to react to the model and to conduct related research.

What follows, then, are revisions in the Expectation Communication Model that have been suggested by several sources. First, changes internal to the model are examined. Second, apparent restrictions on the model's generality are presented. Finally, unanswered questions are offered for future research to explore.

MODIFICATIONS IN THE MODEL

Redefining the Notion of Control

Perhaps the least clear concept in the Expectation Communication Model is the notion of "control." Specifically, the answer to the question "control over what?" has been ambiguous and the present research has suffered because of this lack of clarity.

Earlier Definition of Control. Cooper and Baron (1977) referred to teacher control over students with at least six referents: (1) timing, (2) content, and (3) frequency of interactions, (4) student's likelihood of success, (5) the instance when interactions involving the greatest effort expenditure on the part of the teacher would occur, (6) the point at which teachers personally experienced success and failure. There were at least two themes distinguishing Cooper and Baron's (1977) multiple referents of control. Some referents pertained to aspects of the teacher-student interaction (i.e., frequency, content, timing). Other referents pertained to internal states of the teacher and how capable the teacher was of regulating them (i.e., the distribution of personal efforts, successes, and failures).

The two focuses for the control notion were not initially viewed as problematic, because control over interactions was believed to be causally antecedent to the teachers' ability to regulate personal effort and reinforcement (Cooper, 1977). That is, as a teacher's control over interactions increased, it was believed that teachers' control over personal internal states would increase as well. Similarly, behaviors which were meant to enhance interaction control were thought to simultaneously enhance the teacher's ability to control personal efforts, successes, and failures.

Cooper, Burger, and Seymour (1979; Chapter 5) introduced a scale for measuring teacher-control beliefs (the PCQ), which measured only perceptions of interaction control (i.e., timing, content, and duration). There were several reasons for this single focus. First, it was felt that both teachers and researchers could readily reach agreement about the meaning and significant facets of interaction control. Such agreement about teaching reinforcements and their distribution would be far more difficult to achieve. Second, conversations with teachers had revealed that establishing control over the distribution of personal efforts and reinforcements was only one of several motivations for increasing interaction control. Teachers also reported wanting to spare slow students the experience of public failure and the embarrassment that accompanies it. Finally, and most importantly, teachers' control beliefs would eventually be used to validate the model by relating them to observed classroom-interaction frequencies. It seemed only reasonable to measure those control beliefs most closely related to the instrument's purpose in the investigation.

An examination of the results in Chapters 5 and 6, however, indicate that several simplifying assumptions were inaccurate. These data revealed little association between teacher-interaction control perceptions (as measured by the PCQ) and observed classroom exchanges. In addition, teachers reported extremely high degrees of perceived interaction control over almost all their students. On the other hand, the notion of personal control did appear as an important concept with regard to causal attributions. Teacher citations of teacher-related causes for student performance were associated with the teacher's observed use of affective feedback. Also, the form of the self-attribution and feedback relations was congruent with the communication model predictions: if the teacher felt more involved in successes, the student received freer praise. Likewise, if the teacher felt more responsible for failures, the student received more criticism.

Apparently, then, this study uncovered an instance in which *interaction* control did not relate to behavior in the expected manner, while other perceptions of personal control (measured by teacher-related attributions) did. These results are not presently explainable with the model, but they do suggest ways in which the concept of control might be reformulated.

The Hierarchial Roles of Control Beliefs as Determinants of Teacher Behavior. Instead of being interchangeable, as suggested above, the different referents of control may be related to classroom behavior in a hierarchial manner. Specifically, perceptions of control over interaction parameters may predict teacher feedback until the teacher feels that interaction control over students is "satisfactory." The definition of satisfactory, of course, will vary from teacher to teacher and class to class. Once interaction control is satisfactorily established, the teacher's goal may then shift to establishing control over academic outcomes. For example, in a class composed of students with behavior disorders, the teacher's primary goal may be the establishment of interaction control. For this class the teacher may feel the outcome (success or failure) of instruction cannot be attended to until students work *assigned problems at appropriate times*. In such a class, the teacher may dispense reinforcements dependent on his or her perceived degree of interaction control. If another teacher were assigned to this class (or this teacher assigned a different class), he or she might sense that interaction control was complete enough for the goal of controlling *outcomes* to become salient. The teacher might then reward exchanges which indicate he or she helped bring about a positive outcome and punish exchanges which indicate the teacher caused failure.

In sum, an adequate sense of control over the timing, content and duration of an interaction may be a necessary, *but not sufficient*, cognition for the teacher to sense a strong degree of instructional, or outcome, control. Like the earlier model, this argument suggests that when perceived interaction control is low, perceived control over the outcome of instruction will also be low. However, the earlier model suggested that when interaction control is perceived as high, outcome control would also be seen as high. The new proposal, in contrast, states that high interaction-control beliefs can appear with both high and low perceptions of outcome control.

Advantages of the Hierarchial Formulation. One appealing aspect of the hierarchial notion is that teachers' feelings about their ability to control outcomes is conceptually similar to other researchers' definitions of teacher efficacy beliefs. If the notions of (1) outcome control and (2) control over the distribution of personal efforts, successes, and failures are viewed as synonymous or similar to teacher efficacy beliefs, then a whole new literature becomes relevant to the Expectation Communication Model.

Another appealing aspect of this conceptualization is that it integrates the separate control and attribution findings from the present study. This integration rests on the assumption that the teacher-related attribution category explored in Chapter 6 measures teacher effectiveness beliefs or perceived control over outcomes and personal efforts. Since the teachers in the present study clearly perceived sufficient interaction control, then outcome control would be predicted to relate to behavior. Results on both the PCQ and attribution measure are thus incorporated into the reconceptualization. Of course, the data framed our thinking, so no claim of independent support for this notion is intended.

Finally, the hierarchial formulation for control relations to behavior fits the teacher control links back into the larger expectation communication chain without requiring modification in other stages of the model. Once interaction parameter *and* outcome control have been established, the model suggests that the determinant of teacher feedback becomes the degree of student effort at the task. The control-related links in the model still suggest that high-expectation students (i.e., high-outcome-control students in the present study) will receive more effort-contingent feedback than will low-expectation students.

The Role of Attributions in Face-to-Face Classroom Interactions

Predictions made by the Expectation Communication Model and by attribution theory differ concerning the relations of teacher causal judgments and evaluative feedback. Weiner et al. (1971) argued that effort attributions and feedback should covary: successes seen as caused by strong student effort were predicted to be praised by the teacher while failures perceived to be caused by lack of effort were predicted to be criticized. The Expectation Communication Model, in contrast, predicts that effort is only one contingency for reinforcement in classrooms and it may in fact, be a secondary one [also see Brophy (1981)].

Past Attribution Research. Empirical research conducted in laboratory settings has been uniformly supportive of the attribution theory predictions (Meyer, 1979). However, Cooper and Baron (1979) argued that the supportive results were partly a function of the laboratory setting which produced them. Laboratory experiments typically involved interactions between people who had never previously met and had no anticipation of continuing to interact with one another after the experiment was over. In addition, most laboratory-based attribution research has involved hypothetical teachers and students as opposed to actual educators interacting with children. Cooper and Baron (1979) argued that the laboratory paradigm eliminated aspects of face-to-face classroom interaction which make the control contingency for reinforcement most salient.

It was not argued, however, that earlier attribution-feedback results were complete laboratory artifacts. In fact, Cooper and Baron speculated that this evidence might be highly relevant to the written, noninteractive evaluations which teachers are also asked to perform as part of their pedagogical duties. The grades that students get on individual pieces of written work and report cards may be more effort-related than teacher-control-related. Praise and criticism in these instances will have little effect on the interactions which take place in the classroom.

The data from the present study suggest yet another context in which attribution theory might be relevant. The results seem to support the notion that feedback is effort-contingent when teacher *average feedback use* is at issue. The *between-classroom* data presented in Chapter 6 is consistent with attribution theorizing, though certain predicted relations did not emerge. The average feedback used by teachers in their classes may not be related to the daily requirements of classroom management. Instead, the general level of reinforcement may be related to the general level of effort the class members are believed to expend. Since neither the Expectation Communication Model nor attribution-achievement theory distinguished between the two levels of classroom analysis, this relation was not predicted. However, the emergence of an effort-feedback relation at the between-class level underscores the strong explanatory value of Weiner and colleagues' thinking.

It is equally true, however, that the teachers' distribution of reinforcement *within* a class gave no evidence of being effort-related. Rather, students whose causes implied high teacher control over successes were given more praise than were their classmates. This finding is supportive of the Expectation Communication Model and is *less* supportive of the attribution-theory predictions than the initial model proposed. As first presented, the Expectation Communication Model suggested that effort-feedback relations would exist in classrooms but would be stronger for high- than for low-expectation students. Instead, the data suggested that the effort-feedback relations were negligible for both highs and lows. Classmate differences did emerge when reinforcements were related to the teacher's perceived involvement in success. *Low-expectation students' praise was more contingent than highs' praise on teacher-related causes.* In sum, then, the attributional model may be a satisfactory explanation for written evaluations and the general level of teacher verbal-feedback usage. The Expectation Communication Model may be an appropriate explanation for variation in verbal feedback within classrooms.

The Open-Ended Attribution Questionnaire. The categorization scheme used in this study (Chapter 6) revealed a pattern of attribution usage which is more complex than previous theorizing suggested. In contrast to the dichotomous nature of the original four categories of Weiner et al. (1971), subtle distinctions were found in the stability and internality implications of attributions made by teachers. The open-ended categories also suggested that whereas internality and stability may be central dimensions underlying attributions, other important dimensions, such as implied teacher effectiveness, exist as well. In addition, the results suggested that certain attributions may hold different meanings dependent on who is the referent of the attribution. For example, the attribution category interest in the subject matter might be an unstable characteristic for young students but as students mature this attribution may imply a stable trait. Alternatively, teachers may see themselves as able to stimulate a first grader's interest in mathematics but secondary teachers may feel much less effective at generating interest in a topic area.

Also, the present research suggests that future attribution and behavior studies must ask, "What attributional dimensions relate to behavior in the particular context of interest?" Student-related effort attributions by teachers appear to be associated with reinforcement in some situations, whereas teacher-related effort attributions may be associated with reinforcement in other situations. We should not expect that a given attribution-behavior relation will be universal across contexts. Many dimensions which underlie attributions have been suggested and no doubt more exist. A social context can probably be found in which each attribution dimension influences some behavior. The recognition of context and its importance to social relations requires a careful examination of context characteristics. Such a contextualization of knowledge will not only make theories more complete but will also help generalize theories to real-life situations.

The Role of Student Perceptions in the Expectation Communication Process. With regard to student perceptions of teacher behavior, the question arises about whether it is the objective frequency with which teachers emit behaviors that is of importance in expectation communication or whether this behavioral effect must be mediated by congruent cognitions on the part of the student. Although the Expectation Communication Model did not incorporate this student link, the present study provided two sets of data relevant to it. First, it was found that student perceptions of interaction frequencies exactly paralleled the frequencies said to underlie sustaining expectation effects. The student perceptions were more in line with the model's predictions than were the observed frequencies. It would appear, then, that adding a student perception link to the model would enhance the model's explanatory value. In terms of Figure 1.1, the student perception of teacher behavior link would fit between the teacher use of praise and criticism and student self-efficacy beliefs links.

A second test of the need for the student-perception mediator was attempted in Chapter 8. These data indicated that student self-efficacy beliefs were more strongly related to the frequency of observed classroom interaction than to students' perceptions of interactions. However, differences in the methods used to test each set of relations made this comparison difficult to interpret. It may be best, then, to revise Figure 1.1 to indicate that both the objective and student-perceived teacher behaviors each directly influenced student efficacy beliefs.

RESTRICTIONS ON THE MODEL'S GENERALITY

As each phase of the research was completed, it became increasingly evident that some additional qualifications to the model's generality were needed. The initial formulation of the theory neglected certain contextual restraints on when the model would and would not apply. Three restrictions on the model's generality will be examined.

The Within-Class—Between-Class Distinction. The Expectation Communication Model appears to function primarily at the within-class level. Determining why this is the case requires some speculation, since there are no data in the study to explain the specification. The notion of social comparison is one potential explanatory mechanism (Levine, in press). That is, students' opportunities for comparing their work with other students are more likely to occur within than between classrooms. A likely difference between the two levels of analysis would be the degree to which they are affected by social comparison processes. Students in a particular classroom (within-level) may frequently learn something about themselves through comparison with classmates. Students probably compare themselves less often with other students in other classes with other teachers (between-level). If within-class processes are most likely to be influenced by social comparison among students, social comparison may play an important role in within-class expectation communication. More specifically, it is proposed that expectations within classrooms are communicated by teachers not only through feedback contingencies used with students but also through the students' awareness of differences between feedback to themselves and to other students in the class. Again, there is little hard evidence at present to suggest this is the case. However, the processes that logically appear to be present within classrooms but not between classrooms point strongly to the potential influence of social comparison.

If the present model does not explain expectation communication at the between-class level, what does? Expectations for whole groups of students are certainly communicated and these also play a role in student achievement. No theoretical model guided our thinking on these issues because our awareness of the importance of the between-within distinction grew out of the present research effort. Therefore, a post-hoc explanation must be offered.

The strongest expectation influence at the between-class level may involve Rosenthal's (1974) input factor. The teacher's general expectations for the class may influence the amount of material the teacher presents and the quality of response the teacher is willing to accept before moving on to new material. It is likely that teachers who hold lower expectations for their classrooms as a whole will teach easier lessons, spend less time on rigorous academic activity, and accept less than perfect performance before moving on to new or different material.

In general, the communication of expectations at the whole-class level is probably a very direct process. The variation in the amount of teaching and the quality of acceptable student responses are probably strongly related to whole-class expectations. At the within-class level, however, expectation communication may be much more indirect. The influence of expectations is probably felt through subtle affective behaviors which differ from one student to another, and through the effect this behavior has on students' motivation and relations to figures of authority.

The Effects of Time of the School Year. Another interesting result involved differences in relations dependent upon the time of the school year in which the data was collected. That is, considerably more support was found for the Expectation Communication Model during the fall observation period than during that of winter or spring. The relations between teacher and student behaviors and cognitions fit the model most closely, in fact almost exclusively, during the period covering September and October. The model may thus describe a socialization process that occurs early in the school year when the teacher is most concerned with establishing optimum control. The students learn how to act appropriately through teacher behavior early in the school year. As socialization proceeds, the teacher finds it less and less necessary to communicate the student roles through affect and initiation differences.

If we examine a particular teacher-student relation, the point may become clearer. Assume that a low-achieving student, upon arriving at school, has already been socialized through past educational experience and "knows" that he/she is likely to find the teacher receptive to student initiations only if these occur in private. This student may not receive strong criticism from the teacher and may in fact receive quite a bit of praise during these private interactions. Another low-achieving student, upon arriving in the class, may be considerably less socialized and therefore may behave inappropriately. The teacher will then be more likely to use praise and criticism in order to get this student to behave in the desired manner. As the year progresses, more and more students will come to know how the teacher expects them to behave. As "appropriate" student behavior increases, the teacher will less often use reinforcement to communicate expectations.

The present data demonstrated this diminution of the model's applicability as the year progressed. Of course, certain students are never socialized to teacher expectations and for them, the model may apply throughout the school year. For other students, due perhaps to family crises or changes in peer-group relations, the model may not hold early in the year, but may become more applicable as the year goes on.

The Effects of Social Class.   The present sample of classrooms was drawn from a largely middle-class population in a city dominated by an educational institution. It may be that middle-class classrooms demonstrate the model to a considerably lesser degree than would lower-class classrooms. In lower-class classrooms, interaction control may be more salient because students are probably less socialized to educational environments. We would therefore anticipate greater variance in teachers' perceptions of interaction control over lower-class students. The model relations to interaction control, therefore, would probably have been stronger if the testing were conducted in classrooms in which expectations were generally lower and control beliefs more varied.

FUTURE EXPECTATION RESEARCH

We have examined, critiqued, and revised the research model that guided the present study. Future research will lead to other needed modifications. In this section, topics will be identified upon which new research could be focused.

Other Teacher Beliefs and Cognitions

Teachers' beliefs about the performance levels of individual students and about personal control over students have been examined. It was argued that one model modification involved making a greater distinction between teachers' interaction-control and outcome-control beliefs. These findings also suggest that more attention needs to be paid to other teacher beliefs and cognitions.

Two potential teacher beliefs that might help explain the expectation communication process have been suggested by recent research. Ames (in press) compared teachers who varied in (1) the importance they placed upon being competent and (2) how strongly they believed that teachers could influence student learning. He found that teachers high on these dimensions were more likely (1) to examine the influence of their behavior and (2) to consider changing instructional behavior. In a similar vein, Rohrkemper and Brophy (in press) found that teachers report distinctly different patterns of behavior when classroom problems are perceived as interfering with teacher goals than when they do not. Teachers' intentions in situations where their goals are threatened were characterized by (1) a higher frequency of punishment, (2) restricted use of rationales for behavior, and (3) emphasis upon short-term control of student behavior.

It may also be fruitful to examine how teacher performance beliefs and other teacher cognitions (e.g., norms, preferences) interact with one another. For example, a teacher who holds a high expectation for a shy student may treat that student differently from one who is highly regarded but not shy. Teachers have preferences for particular student personality types and several researchers have found that teachers' preferences may be associated with differential behavior (Brophy and Evertson, 1981; Carew and Lightfoot, 1979; Levine and Mann, Note 9.1). These preferences may interact with teacher beliefs about student potential.

Future expectation research should measure other beliefs in conjunction with performance expectations and should consider how these cognitions influence teacher behavior. In addition to those mentioned above, researchers might identify other important teacher cognitions through systematic but open-ended interviews and then verify the role of these beliefs through classroom observation.

Within-Class Groups of Students

The present research only sampled behavior when the entire class was engaged in one activity or when students worked individually. No attention was paid to groupings of students within classrooms but these assignments may have important effects on student achievement. Weinstein (1976) reported that the reading group in which the student was placed explained 25 percent of the variance in midyear achievement over and above students' initial readiness scores. It would appear that placement into high- and low-reading groups may serve to communicate expectancy effects and to affect student performance in some classrooms (also see Rist, 1970).

Grouping may explain variance in behavior as well. Confrey and Good (Note 9.2) found that eighth-grade students in high and low groups in mathematics and English classes received distinct teacher behavior. For example, the English teacher reported "enjoying" the high group more than the low. This attitude was associated with more general contact with highs than lows. Furthermore, lows received reading assignments that were less interesting and demanding than those assigned to highs.

Composition of Classes

Teachers' expectations and behavior toward individual students may be influenced by teachers' reactions to other students or to the class generally. Teachers who hold a favorable expectation for the class as a whole may be less susceptible to communicating expectation effects because they are motivated (and perhaps because they have the time) to look for signs of student progress. Teachers who feel that a class as a whole is controllable may shift their focus with individual problem students from interaction concerns to outcome concerns more quickly than will teachers who perceive a class as less teachable.

In a demonstration of class composition effects on individual learning, Berkerman and Good (1981) found that the ratio of high- to low-achieving students in a class was associated with individual student-achievement change. Specifically, they found that in classes where low-achieving students were taught with many high-achieving students, lows performed better than they did in classrooms where lows were taught with a higher percent of other low achievers.

Beckerman and Good did not measure teacher expectations, so the relation between teacher beliefs and different combinations of students was not tested. The program of research presented in this book did examine whole-class expectations, defined as the sum of individual student expectations, but did not measure the distribution of expectations within classes. Future expectation research should explore the reciprocal effects of classroom-composition variables and individual teacher expectations.

Students as Independent Variables

The need for more attention to student variables was mentioned earlier in the chapter. This treatment viewed student cognitions as mediators of teacher behavior and instruction. However, student perceptions and behaviors need to be incorporated into future expectation studies as independent variables as well as mediating variables.

Spencer Hall (1981) has illustrated how students sometimes control teacher thoughts. She found that teachers nominated some students for citizenship awards even though they often engaged in blatant misbehavior. These students had the ability to misbehave at times when the teacher was not watching. Good (Note 9.3) observed the same junior high science teacher in two classes. The instructor had described one of the classes as easy but "boring" to teach and the other as easy but "fun" to teach. The fun class received more content than did the boring class, which seemed to be owing to greater student initiative in question asking in the fun class. Also, Copeland (1979) found that a student-teacher who taught differently from the regular teacher met with student behaviors that eventually forced the student-teacher to teach as the regular teacher had.

A study by Feldman and Prohaska (1979) demonstrated the importance of the students' expectations for the teacher. They had students receive a lesson from a teacher whom they expected to be either effective or ineffective. The students' attitudes toward the teacher, their performance on postexperimental tests, and their nonverbal behavior during the lesson differed dependent on their preconceptions of how effective the teacher would be. In a second experiment, students who emitted positive nonverbal behaviors toward teachers were found to elicit significantly more positive attitudes and behaviors from teachers than did students who emitted negative nonverbal behaviors.

Each of these works points out the interdependence of teachers and students and the importance of examining both the teacher and the student as active communicators with self-perceptions based partly on the responses of the other. A promising strategy for uncovering the phenomenological perspective of students would appear to involve detailed interviews (e.g., Confrey, Note 9.4) coupled with classroom observation. Fortunately, several such efforts have recently been reported (Blumenfeld et al., in press; Confrey, Note 9.4; Good, Note 9.5; Rohrkemper, Note 9.6; Tikunoff and Mergendoller, Note 9.7; Weinstein et al., Note 9.8).

Structural and Curriculum Variables

Structure. Two aspects of classroom structure, within-class groupings and student composition, were mentioned above. Teacher behavior is also influenced by other structural variables. For example, teachers are found to use more negative feedback in classrooms with more large-group teaching and teacher selection of goals (Blumenfeld et al., 1979; Solomon and Kendall, 1975). Classroom organization also influences the opportunities students have to learn from other students (Bossert, 1979). Students' opportunities for working with other students can be increased by using small work groups (e.g., Slavin, in press). There are also data to suggest that cooperative, interdependent assignments can affect friendship patterns and student perceptions of ability (Aronson et al., 1978; Rosenholtz and Wilson, 1980).

More directly related to expectation effects is a study by Germano and Peterson (1982). They found that teaching in self-contained versus individualized structures was associated with (1) differential salience of particular student characteristics (e.g., sociability, achievement), and (2) teacher use of information to make instructional decisions. There are also arguments and data which suggest that the form of particular learning *tasks* can influence student and teacher behavior (Borko et al., 1979; Doyle, Note 9.9). It will be important in the future to study how structural variations affect the relations between expectations and classroom behavior.

Curriculum. Leinhardt et al. (1979) found that subject matter was associated with differential teacher behavior toward boys and girls. In particular, girls had more academic contacts with teachers during reading, whereas boys had more during mathematics. Whether these gender-by-subject-interaction patterns are primarily owing to teachers' beliefs and behaviors or to student factors is not clear. Such findings do reflect the need to study how subject matter may mediate or affect the expectation communication process.

It also appears that teachers vary their behavior when teaching different subject matter to the *same* group of students (Soltz, Note 9.10). There is also evidence that different teacher conceptions of subject matter relate to teaching behavior in some instances (Shavelson, 1980). However, how subject-matter beliefs *interact* with teachers' performance expectations for individuals or groups of students is largely unexplored and research is needed in this area.

Curriculum variables also appear to have the potential for affecting the beliefs and behavior of students. Unfortunately, there has been very little research relating subject matter to student-performance expectations. Future research might determine whether students hold different expectations for their performance in math and reading and whether these subject-matter beliefs affect the way they present themselves to teachers.

Finer Segments of Behavior

Studying restricted segments of classroom life would appear to have great potential for uncovering the roots of expectation effects. By obtaining the immediate reactions of teacher and student to classroom events, finer and more immediate comparisons could be made. For example, in the present research a general questionnaire (the IAR) was used to measure students' beliefs about personal control of learning outcomes. A restricted but more sensitive measure of student effort might be the number of problems attempted on a particular assignment. Attention to this type of student behavior may provide a sensitive key for establishing the motivational consequences of teacher feedback. A focus on fine-units behavior would also allow for the examination of the effects of student behavior on teachers (e.g., to see if teachers' planning for subsequent lessons is informed by awareness of students' performance on a particular lesson). Future research of this sort would likely illustrate the reciprocal effects of students and teachers and enrich our understanding of curriculum and context variables as well (Brophy, 1979; Stipek and Weisz, 1981).

Multiple Teachers

In Chapter 4, it was shown that teachers behaved differently in the fall than in the spring (see also Evertson and Veldman, 1981). Another type of within-year longitudinal model has been suggested by Good (1981). He points out that some slow learners have remedial math, reading, and/or speech teachers while other students remain with one instructor. Although there are no data to describe if and how remedial teachers differ from regular classroom teachers in their instructional behavior, the presence of multiple teachers means lows will likely encounter variable teacher expectations and behavior. Future research could profitably focus upon the effects of multiple teachers upon student performance and perceptions.

Longitudinal Research. More longitudinal research also needs to be conducted across consecutive school years. Classroom participants have a long history of schooling, but the influence of this experience is typically excluded from educational field studies. In any given year it is impossible to determine whether teacher and student behavior is a reaction to current events or to some earlier experience.

Some students may move from one classroom or grade to another and receive comparable teacher-performance expectations, whereas other students may experience major discontinuities in teacher expectations and behavior. Good (1981) has argued that lows may receive more varied teaching behavior from year to year than do highs, because teachers in general agree less about how to respond when new tasks are not learned quickly. The hypothesis of greater variation in teacher behavior toward lows than highs, however, has not been tested directly. No large-scale systematic research has followed the same group of students over consecutive years. If lows do receive more discontinuities in teacher behavior, it seems plausible that such differences might contribute to a passive learning style for lows. It would be unfortunate if students who have the least adaptive capacity are asked to make the greatest adjustments as they move from class to class.

Longitudinal research could determine the frequency of such discontinuities and could examine how students accommodate these differences when they occur. Obviously, certain discontinuities in teacher expectations across years may have useful academic effects upon students. The argument here is not that such effects are generally negative but that studying such effects and evaluating their impact on different types of students is an important goal for research.

Conclusion

In this chapter we have tried to take a critical look at our work and theorizing. It is not unusual for social scientists to find that their original thinking was simplistic. Therefore, we are not surprised to find that reality is far more complex than is our thinking. We hope that the proposed model revisions prove viable and bring the model into a closer correspondence with actual classroom events. We also hope that the model will become more specific in the future and that aspects of classroom life to which the model is not relevant will be more clearly delineated. The future research we suggested was chosen with these goals in mind.

Reference Notes

1.1 Brattesani, K., Weinstein, R., Marshall, H., and Middlestadt, S. *Using student perceptions of teacher behavior to predict student outcomes*. Paper presented at the annual meeting of the American Educational Research Association, Los Angeles, April 1981.

1.2 Evertson, C., Brophy, J., and Good, T. *Communication of teacher expectations: Second grade*. Austin, TX: University of Texas at Austin, Research and Development Center for Teacher Education report 92, 1973.

3.1 Soar, R., and Soar, R. *Setting variables, classroom interactions, and multiple pupil outcomes*. National Institute of Education Project 6–0432, 1978.

5.1 Medinnus, G., and Unruh, R. *Teacher expectations and verbal communication*. Paper presented at the annual meeting of the Western Psychological Association, 1971.

6.1 Rosenbaum, R. *A dimensional analysis of the perceived causes of success and failure*. Unpublished dissertation, University of California, Los Angeles, 1972.

6.2 Marland, P. *A study of teachers' interactive thoughts*. Unpublished dissertation, University of Alberta, Alberta, 1977.

7.1 Ehman, L. *A comparison of three sources of classroom data: Teachers, students, and systematic observation*. Paper presented at the annual meeting of the American Educational Research Association, 1970.

9.1 Levine, H., and Mann, K. *The "negotiations" of classroom lessons and its relevance for teachers' decision-making*. Paper presented at the annual meeting of the American Educational Research Association, Los Angeles, April 1981.

9.2 Confrey, J., and Good, T. *A view from the back of the classroom: Integrating student and teacher perspectives of content with observational, clinical interviews*, in progress.

9.3 Good, T. *Classroom research: Past and Future*. Center for Research in Social Behavior Technical Report 207, University of Missouri, Columbia, 1980

9.4 Confrey, J. *Using clinical interviews to explore students' understanding*. Paper presented at the annual meeting of the American Educational Research Association, Los Angeles, April 1981.

9.5 Good, T. *Listening to students talk about classrooms*. Paper presented at the annual meeting of the American Educational Research Association, Los Angeles, April 1981.

9.6 Rohrkemper, M. *Classroom perspectives study: An investigation of differential student perceptions of classroom events.* An unpublished dissertation, Michigan State University, East Lansing, Michigan, 1981.

9.7 Tikunoff, W., and Mergendoller, J. et al. *Integrating student perspectives with ecological theory*, in progress.

9.8 Weinstein, R., Marshall, H., Middlestadt, S., Brattesani, K., and Sharp, L. *Student perceptions of differential teacher treatment.* N.I.E. Final Report (NIE-G-79-0078), University of California, Berkeley, 1981.

9.9 Doyle, W. *Student mediating responses in teaching effectiveness.* N.I.E. Final Report (NIE-G-76-0099), North Texas State University, Denton, Texas, 1980.

9.10 Soltz, D. *The various teacher: Subject matter, style, and strategy in the primary classroom.* Paper presented at the annual meeting of the American Educational Research Association, April 1976.

References

Abramson, L., Seligman, M. & Teasdale, J. Learned helplessness in humans: Critique and reformulation. *Journal of Abnormal Psychology*, 1978, *87*, 49–74.

Ames, R. Teacher value perspectives. In J. Levine and M. Wang (eds.), *Teacher and student perceptions: Implications for learning*. Morristown, NJ: Erlbaum, in press.

Andrews, G., and Debus, R. Persistence and the causal perception of failure: Modifying cognitive attributions. *Journal of Educational Psychology*, 1978, *70*, 154–166.

Aronson, E., Blaney, N., Stephan, C., Sikes, J., and Snapp, M. *The jigsaw puzzle*. Beverly Hills, CA: Sage, 1978.

Atkinson, J. *An introduction to motivation*. Princeton, NJ: Van Nostrand, 1964.

Babad, E. Personality correlates of susceptibility to biasing information. *Journal of Personality and Social Psychology*, 1979, *37*, 195–202.

Babad, E., Inbar, J., and Rosenthal, R. Teacher judgment of students' potential as a function of teachers' susceptibility to biasing information. *Journal of Personality and Social Psychology*, 1982, *42*, 541–547.

Bandura, A. Self-efficacy: Toward a unifying theory of behavior change. *Psychological Review*, 1977, *84*, 191–215.

———, Inbar, J., and Rosenthal, R. Pygmalion galatea and the golem: Investigations of biased and unbiased teachers. *Journal of Educational Psychology*, in press.

Bank, B., Biddle, B., and Good, T. Sex roles, classroom instruction, and reading achievement. *Journal of Educational Psychology*, 1980, *72*, 119–132.

Barr, R., and Dreeban, R. Instruction in classrooms. In L. Shulman (ed.), *Review of research in education*, *No. 5*. Itasca, IL: Peacock, 1977.

Bar-Tal, D. Attributional analysis of achievement-related behavior. *Review of Educational Research*, 1978, *48*, 259–271.

———, and Darom, E. Pupils' attributions of success and failure. *Child Development*, 1979, *50*, 264–267.

———, and Saxe, L. *Social psychology of education*: Theory and research. New York: Halsted, 1978.

Beckerman, T., and Good, T. The classroom ratio of high- and low-aptitude students and its effect on achievement. *American Educational Research Journal*, 1981, *18*, 317–327.

Beez, W. Influence of biased psychological reports on teacher behavior and pupil performance. In M. W. Miles and W. W. Charters, Jr. (eds.), *Learning in social settings*. Boston: Allyn and Bacon, 1970.

Biddle, B. *Role theory: Expectations, identities and behaviors*. New York: Academic, 1979.

Blumenfeld, P., Hamilton, V., Bossert, S., Wessels, K., and Meece, J. Teacher talk and student thought: Socialization into the student role. In J. Levine and M. Wang (eds.), *Teacher and student perceptions: Implications for learning*. Morristown, NJ: Erlbaum, in press.

Blumenfeld, P., Hamilton, V., Wessels, K., and Faulkner, D. Teaching responsibility to first graders. *Theory Into Practice*, 1979, *18*, 174–180.

Borg, W. Teacher coverage of academic content and pupil achievement. *Journal of Educational Psychology*, 1979, *71*, 635–645.

Borko, H., Cone, R., Russo, N., and Shavelson, R. Teachers' decision-making. In P. Peterson and H. Walberg (eds.), *Research on teaching: Concepts, findings and implications*. Berkeley, CA: McCutchan., 1979.

Bossert, S. *Task and social relationships in classrooms: A study of classroom organization and its consequences*. American Sociological Association, Arnold & Caroline Rose Monograph Series. New York: Cambridge University Press, 1979.

Brannon, R. Attitudes and the prediction of behavior. In B. Seidenberg and A. Snadowsky (eds.), *Social psychology: An introduction*. New York: Free Press, 1976.

Braun, C. Teacher expectation: Socio-psychological dynamics. *Review of Educational Research*, 1976, *46*, 185–213.

Brechner, M., and Denmark, F. Internal-external locus of control and verbal fluency. *Psychological Reports*, 1969, *25*, 707–710.

Brophy, J. Teacher behavior and its effects. *Journal of Educational Psychology*, 1979, *71*, 733–750.

———, Teacher praise: A functional analysis. *Review of Educational Research*, 1981, *51*, 5–32.

———, and Evertson, C. *Student characteristics and teaching*. New York: Longman, 1981.

———, and Good, T. *Teacher-child dyadic interaction: A manual for coding behavior*. Austin: The Research and Development Center for Teacher Education, The University of Texas, 1969.

———, and Good, T. Brophy-Good system (Teacher-child dyadic interaction). In A. Simon & E. Boyer (eds.), *Mirrors for behavior*. Philadelphia: Research for Better Schools, Inc., 1970a.

———, and ———. Teachers' communication of differential expectations for children's classroom performance: Some behavioral data. *Journal of Educational Psychology*, 1970b, *61*, 365–374.

———, and ———. *Teacher-student relationships: Causes and consequences*. New York: Holt, 1974.

Burstein, L. The analysis of multilevel data in educational research and evaluation. In D. Berliner (ed.), *Review of Research in Education, Vol. 8*. Washington, D.C.: American Educational Research Association, 1980.

———, and Smith, I. Choosing the appropriate unit for investigating school effects. *Australian Journal of Education*, 1978, *21* (1), 65–79.

Carew, J., and Lightfoot, S. *Beyond bias.* Cambridge, MA: Harvard University Press, 1979.

Chaikin, A., Sigler, E., and Derlega, V. Nonverbal mediators of teacher expectancy effects. *Journal of Personality and Social Psychology*, 1974, *30* (1), 144–149.

Claiborn, W. Expectancy effects in the classroom: A failure to replicate. *Journal of Educational Psychology*, 1969, *60*, 377–383.

Clark, K. Educational stimulation of racially disadvantaged children. In A. H. Passow (ed.), *Education in depressed areas.* New York: Teachers College, Columbia University, 1963.

Cohen, J. A coefficient of agreement of nominal scales. *Educational and Psychological Measurement*, 1960, *20*, 37–46.

Cooper, H. Controlling personal rewards: Professional teachers differential use of feedback and the effects of feedback on the student's motivation to perform. *Journal of Educational Psychology*, 1977, *69* (4), 419–427.

———, Pygmalion grows up: A model for teacher expectation communication and performance influence. *Review of Educational Research*, 1979, *49*, 389–410.

———, Communication of teacher expectations to students. In J. Levine and M. Wang (eds.), *Teacher and student perceptions: Implications for learning.* Hillsdale, N.J.: Erlbaum, in press.

———, and Baron, R. Academic expectations and attributed responsibility as predictors of professional teachers' reinforcement behavior. *Journal of Educational Psychology*, 1977, *69* (4), 409–418.

———, and ———. Academic expectations, attributed responsibility, and teachers' reinforcement behavior: A suggested integration of conflicting literatures. *Journal of Educational Psychology*, 1979, *1*, 274–277.

———, and Burger, J. How teachers explain students' academic performance: A categorization of free response academic attributions. *American Educational Research Journal*, 1980, *17* (1), 95–109.

———, Burger, J., and Good, T. Gender differences in the academic locus of control beliefs of young children. *Journal of Personality and Social Psychology*, 1981, *40* (3), 562–572.

———, Burger, J., and Seymour, G. Classroom context and student ability as influences on teacher personal and success expectations. *American Educational Research Journal*, 1979, *16* (2), 189–196.

———, Hinkel, G., and Good, T. Teachers' beliefs about interaction control and their observed behavioral correlates. *Journal of Educational Psychology*, 1980, *72* (3), 345–354.

———, and Lowe, C. Task information and attributions for academic performance by professional teachers and role players. *Journal of Personality*, 1977, *45* (4), 469–483.

Copeland, W. Student teachers and cooperating teachers: An ecological relationship. *Theory Into Practice*, 1979, *3*, 194–199.

Cornbleth, C., Davis, O., and Button, C. Expectations for pupil achievement and teacher-pupil interaction. *Social Education*, 1974, *38* (1), 54–58.

Corno, L. A hierarchial analysis of selected naturally occurring aptitude-treatment interactions in the third grade. *American Educational Research Journal*, 1979, *16* (4), 391–409.

Crandall, V. C., Katkovsky, W., and Crandall, V. J. Children's beliefs in their own control of reinforcements in intellectual-academic achievement situations. *Child Development*, 1965, *36*, 91–109.

Crano, W., & Mellon, P. Causal influences of teacher's expectations on children's academic performance: A cross-lagged panel analysis. *Journal of Educational Psychology*, 1978, *70* (1), 39–49.

Cronbach, L. *Research on classrooms and schools: Formulation of questions, design and analysis.* Stanford Evaluation Consortium, ERIC Document No. ED 135 801, Stanford University, Stanford, CA, 1976.

Dalton, W. The relations between classroom interaction and teacher ratings of pupils: An explanation of one means by which a teacher may communicate her expectancies. *Peabody Papers in Human Development*, 1969, *1* (6).

Darley, J. M., and Fazio, R. H. Expectancy confirmation processes arising in the social interaction sequence. *American Psychologist*, 1980, *35*, 867–881.

deCharms, R. *Personal causation.* New York: Academic, 1968.

Dunkin, M., and Biddle, B. *The study of teaching.* New York: Holt, 1974.

Dusek, J. Do teachers bias children's learning? *Review of Educational Research*, 1975, *45*, 661–684.

Dweck, C., Davidson, W., Nelson, S., and Enna, B. Sex differences in learned helplessness: II. The contingencies of evaluative feedback in the classroom and III. An experimental analysis. *Developmental Psychology*, 1978, *14*, 268–276.

———, and Gilliard, D. Expectancy statements as determinants of reactions to failure: Sex differences in persistence and expectancy change. *Journal of Personality and Social Psychology*, 1975, *32*, 1077–1084.

———, Goetz, T., and Strauss, N. Sex differences in learned helplessness: IV. An experimental and naturalistic study of failure generalization and its mediators. *Journal of Personality and Social Psychology*, 1980, *38*, 441–452.

———, and Reppucci, D. Learned helplessness and reinforcement responsibility in children. *Journal of Personality and Social Psychology*, 1973, *25* (1), 109–116.

Entwisle, D., and Hayduk, L. *Too great expectations: The academic outlook of young children.* Baltimore: The John Hopkins, 1978.

———, and Webster, M. Raising children's performance expectations. *Social Science Research*, 1972, *1*, 147–158.

Evertson, C., Brophy, J., and Good, T. *Communication of teacher expectations: First grade.* Research and Development Center for Teacher Education report 91, The University of Texas at Austin, 1972.

———, and Veldman, D. Changes over time and process measures of classroom behavior. *Journal of Educational Psychology*, 1981, *73*, 156–163.

Feldman, R., and Prohaska, T. The student as pygmalion: Effect of student expectation on the teacher. *Journal of Educational Psychology*, 1979, *71*, 485–493.

Feshbach, N. Student teacher preferences for elementary school pupils varying in personality characteristics. *Journal of Educational Psychology*, 1969, *60*, 126–132.

Firestone, G., and Brody, N. Longitudinal investigation of teacher-student interactions and their relation to academic performance. *Journal of Educational Psychology*, 1975, *67* (4), 544–550.

Fleming, E., and Anttonen, R. Teacher expectancy or my fair lady. *American Educational Research Journal*, 1971, *8*, 241–252.

Frick, T., and Semmel, M. Observer agreement and reliabilities of classroom observational measures. *Review of Educational Research*, 1978, *48* (1), 157–184.

Frieze, I. H. Causal attributions and information seeking to explain success and failure. *Journal of Research in Personality*, 1976, *10*, 293–305.

Germano, M., and Peterson, P. A comparison of individually guided education (IGE) teachers' and non-IGE teachers' use of student characteristics in making instructional decisions. *Elementary School Journal*, 1982, *82*, 319–328.

Good, T. Which pupils do teachers call on? *Elementary School Journal*, 1970, *70*, 190–198.

———. Classroom expectations: Teacher-pupil interactions. In J. McMillan (ed.), *The social psychology of school learning*. New York: Academic, 1980.

———. Teacher expectations and student perceptions: A decade of research. *Educational Leadership*, 1981, *38*, 415–422.

———, Biddle, B. & Brophy, J. *Teachers make a difference*. New York: Holt, Rinehart and Winston, 1975.

———, and Brophy, J. Teacher-child dyadic interactions: A new method of classroom observation, *Journal of Social Psychology*, 1970, *8* (2), 131–138.

———, and Brophy, J. Analyzing classroom interaction: A more powerful alternative. *Educational Technology*, 1971, *11*, 36–40.

———, & Brophy, J. *Looking in classrooms*. New York: Harper & Row, 1973.

———, & Brophy, J. *Educational psychology: A realistic approach* (2d Ed.). New York: Holt, 1980.

———, Sikes, J., and Brophy, J. Effects of teacher sex and student sex on classroom interaction. *Journal of Educational Psychology*, 1973, *65*, 74–87.

Goodlad, J., Klein, M., and Associates. *Behind the classroom door*. Worthington: C. A. Jones, 1970.

Gustafsson, C. *Classroom interaction: A study of pedagogical roles in the teaching process*. Stockholm, Gruppen, 1977.

Heider, F. *The psychology of interpersonal relations*. New York: Wiley, 1958.

Hook, C., and Rosenshine, B. Accuracy of teacher reports of their classroom behavior. *Review of Educational Research*, 1979, *49*, 1–12.

Humphreys, L., and Stubbs, J. A longitudinal analysis of teacher expectations, student expectations, and student's achievement. *Journal of Educational Measurement*, 1977, *14*, 261–270.

Jackson, P. *Life in classrooms*. New York: Holt, 1968.

Jeter, J. Can teacher expectations function as self-fulfilling prophecies? *Contemporary Education*, 1975, *96* (3), 161–165.

Jones, V. The influence of teacher-student introversion, achievement, and similarity on teacher-student dyadic classroom interactions, doctoral dissertation, University of Texas at Austin. *Dissertation Abstracts International*, 1972, 6205–A.

Kennelly, R., and Kinley, S. Perceived contingency of teacher administered reinforcements and academic performance of boys. *Psychology in the Schools*, 1975, *12*, 449–453.

Kester, S., and Letchworth, G. Communication of teacher expectations and their effects on achievement and attitudes of secondary school students. *Journal of Educational Research*, 1972, *66*, 51–55.

Koopman, C., and Newtson, D. Level of analysis in the perception of ongoing instruction: An exploratory study. *Journal of Educational Psychology*, 1981, *73*, 212–223.

Kukla, A. Attributional determinants of achievement-related behavior. *Journal of Personality and Social Psychology*, 1972, *21*, 166–174.

Langer, E., and Rodin, J. The effects of choice and enhanced personal responsibility for the aged: A field experiment in an institutional setting. *Journal of Personality and Social Psychology*, 1976, *34*, 191–198.

Lefcourt, H., Hoggs, E., Struthers, S., and Holmes, C. Causal attributions as a function of locus of control, initial confidence and performance outcomes. *Journal of Personality and Social Psychology*, 1975, *32,* 391–397.

Leinhardt, G., Seewald, A., and Engel, M. Learning what's taught: Sex differences in instruction. *Journal of Educational Psychology*, 1979, *71* (4), 432–439.

Levine, J. Social comparison. In J. Levine and M. Wang (eds.), *Teacher and student perceptions: Implications for learning.* Morristown, NJ: Erlbaum, in press.

Lindquist, E. *Design and analysis of experiments in psychology and education.* Boston: Houghton Mifflin, 1953.

Luce, S., and Hoge, R. Relations among teacher rankings, pupil-teacher interactions and academic achievement: A test of the teacher expectancy hypothesis. *American Educational Research Journal*, 1978, *15* (4), 489–500.

McDonald, F., and Elias, P. *The effects of teacher performance on pupil learning.* Beginning Teacher Evaluation Study: Phase II, final report: Vol. 1. Princeton, NJ: Educational Testing Service, 1976.

McMillan, J. (ed.). *The social psychology of school learning.* New York: Academic, 1980.

Meichenbaum, C., Bowers, K., and Ross, R. A behavioral analysis of teacher-expectancy effect. *Journal of Personality and Social Psychology*, 1969, *13*, 306–316.

Merton, R. K. The self-fulfilling prophecy. *Antioch Review*, 1948, *8*, 193–210.

Merton, R. K. *Social theory and social structure.* New York: Free Press, 1957.

Meyer, W. Academic expectations, attributed responsibility, and teachers' reinforcement behavior: A comment on Cooper and Baron, with some additional data. *Journal of Educational Psychology*, 1979, *71*, 269–273.

Myers, J. *Fundamentals of experimental design* (2d ed.). New York: McGraw-Hill, 1972.

———. *Fundamentals of experimental design* (3d Ed.). Boston: Allyn and Bacon, 1979.

Nunnally, J. *Psychometric theory* (2d ed.). New York: McGraw-Hill, 1978.

Orvis, B., Kelley, H., and Butler, D. Attributional conflict in young couples. In J. Harvey, W. G. Ickes, and R. F. Kidd (eds.), *New directions in attribution research* (vol. 1). Hillsdale, NJ: Erlbaum, 1976.

Page, E. Statistically recapturing the richness within the classroom. *Psychology in the Schools*, 1975, *12* (3), 339–344.

Petrinovich, L. Probabilistic functionalism: A conception of research method. *American Psychologist*, 1979, *34* (3), 373–390.

Phares, E. *Locus of control in personality.* Morristown, NJ: General Learning Press, 1976.

Poynor, H. Selecting units of analysis. In G. Borich (ed.), *Evaluating educational programs and products*. Engelwood Cliffs, NJ: Educational Technological Press, 1974.

Riemer, B. Influence of causal beliefs on affect and expectancy. *Journal of Personality and Social Psychology*, 1975, *31*, 1163–1167.

Rist, R. Student social class and teacher expectations. The self-fulfilling prophecy in ghetto education. *Harvard Educational Review*, 1970, *40*, 411–451.

Rohrkemper, M. Teacher self-assessment. In D. Duke (ed.), *Helping teachers manage classrooms*, ASCD, Volume on Classroom Management, Alexandria, VA: Association for Supervision and Curriculum Development, 1982.

————, and Brophy, J. Teachers' thinking about problem students. In J. Levine and M. Wang (eds.), *Teacher and student perceptions: Implications for learning*. Morristown, NJ: Erlbaum, in press.

Rosenholtz, S., and Wilson, B. The effect of classroom structure on shared perceptions of ability. *American Educational Research Journal*, 1980, *17*, 75–82.

Rosenthal, R. *On the social psychology of the self-fulfilling prophecy: Further evidence for Pygmalion effects and their mediating mechanisms*. New York: MSS Modular, 1974.

————. *Experimenter effects in behavioral research* (2d ed.). New York: Irvington, 1976.

————, and Jacobson, L. *Pygmalion in the classroom: Teacher expectation and pupils' intellectual development*. New York: Holt, 1968.

Rothbart, M., Dalfen, S., and Barrett, R. Effects of teacher's expectancy on student-teacher interaction. *Journal of Educational Psychology*, 1971, *62*, 49–54.

Rowe, M. Wait time and rewards as instructional variables, their influence on language, logic and fate control. *Journal of Research in Science*, 1974, *11* (4), 291–308.

Rubovitz, R., and Maehr, M. Pygmalion analyzed: Toward an explanation of the Rosenthal-Jacobson findings. *Journal of Personality and Social Psychology*, 1971 *19*, 197–203.

Salomon, G. Self-fulfilling and self-sustaining prophecies and the behaviors that realize them. *American Psychologist*, 1981, *36*, 1452–1453.

Sarbin, T., and Allen, V. Increasing participation in a natural group setting: A preliminary report. *Psychological Record*, 1968, *18*, 1–7.

Schrank, W. The labeling effect of ability grouping. *Journal of Educational Research*, 1968, *62*, 51–52.

————. A further study of the labeling effect of ability grouping. *Journal of Educational Research*, 1970, *63*, 358–360.

Seligman, M. *Helplessness: On depression, development and death*. New York: Freeman, 1975.

Shavelson, R. *Research on teachers' pedagogical thoughts, judgments, decisions and behavior*. Washington, D.C.: National Institute of Education, 1980.

Slavin, R. A case study of psychological research affecting classroom practice: Student team learning. *Elementary School Journal*, in press.

Smith, M. Meta-analysis of research on teacher expectations. *Evaluation in Education*, 1980, *4*, 53–55.

Snedecor, G., and Cochran, W. *Statistical methods* (6th ed.). Ames, IA: Iowa State University Press, 1974.

Snow, R. Unfinished pygmalion. *Contemporary Psychology*, 1969, *14*, 197–199.

Solomon, D., and Kendall, A. Teachers' perceptions of and reactions to misbehavior in traditional and open classrooms. *Journal of Educational Psychology*, 1975, *67*, 528–530.

Spencer Hall, D. Looking behind the teacher's back. *Elementary School Journal*, 1981, *81* (5), 281–289.

Squire, J., and Applebee R. *A study of English programs in selected high schools which consistently educate outstanding students in English*. Urbana: University of Illinois Press, 1966.

Steiner, D. Perceived freedom. In L. Berkowitz (ed.), *Advances in experimental social psychology*, vol. 5. New York: Academic, 1970.

Stipek, D., and Weisz, J. Perceived personal control and academic achievement. *Review of Educational Research*, 1981, *51* (1), 101–137.

Sutherland, A., and Goldschmid, M. Negative teacher expectations and IQ change in children with superior intellectual potential. *Child Development*, 1974, *45* (3), 852–856.

Taylor, M. Race, sex, and the expression of self-fulfilling prophecies in a laboratory teaching situation. *Journal of Personality and Social Psychology*, 1979, *37*, 897–912.

Thomas, W., and Thomas, D. *The child in America*. New York: Knopf, 1928.

Uguroglu, M., and Walberg, H. Motivation and achievement: A quantitative synthesis. *American Educational Research Journal*, 1979, *16*, 375–389.

Weiner, B. *Achievement motivation and attribution theory*. Morristown, NJ: General Learning Press, 1974.

———. An attributional approach for educational psychology. In L. Shulman (ed.), *Review of research in education* (vol. 4). Itasca, IL: Peacock, 1977a.

———. Attribution and affect: Comments on Sohn's critique. *Journal of Educational Psychology*, 1977b, *69*, 506–511.

———, Frieze, I., Kukla, A., Reed, L., Rest, S., and Rosenbaum, R. *Perceiving the causes of success and failure*. Morristown, NJ: General Learning Press, 1971.

———, Russell, D., and Lerman, D. Affective consequences of causal ascriptions. In J. H. Harvey, W. J. Ickes, and R. F. Kidd (eds.), *New directions in attribution research* (vol. 2). Hillsdale, NJ: Erlbaum, 1978.

Weinstein, R. Reading group membership in first grade: Teacher behaviors and pupil experience over time. *Journal of Educational Psychology*, 1976, *68*, 103–116.

———, and Middlestadt, S. Student perceptions of teacher interactions with male high and low achievers. *Journal of Educational Psychology*, 1975, *71* (4), 421–431.

West, C., and Anderson, T. The question of preponderant causation in teacher expectancy research. *Review of Educational Research*, 1976, *46*, 185–213.

Index